REATA

LEGENDARY TEXAS CUISINE

MIKE MICALLEF

With Julie Hatch and John DeMers

Photography by Laurie Smith

TEN SPEED PRESS
Berkeley

All rights reserved. Published in the United States by Ten
Speed Press, an imprint of the Crown Publishing Group, a
division of Random House, Inc., New York.
www.crownpublishing.com
www.tenspeed.com

Ten Speed Press and the Ten Speed Press colophon are
registered trademarks of Random House, Inc.

Library of Congress Cataloging-in-Publication Data
Micallef, Michael.
Reata : legendary Texas cuisine / Michael Micallef.
        p. cm.
Includes bibliographical references and index.
1. Cookery, American—Southwestern style. 2. Cookery—
Texas. 3. Reata Restaurant. I. Title.
TX715.2.S69M52 2009
641.59764—dc22

                              2008014635

ISBN-13: 978-1-58008-906-7
Printed in China

Jacket and text design by Toni Tajima
Principal photography by Laurie Smith
Principal food styling by Erica McNeish
Additional images were contributed by the following:
     Gil Bartee: pages 67, 115
     Ken Davis: pages xxi, 21, 58, 67, and 101
     Rhonda Hole: pages xvii, xviii, 4, 23, 51, 153, and 154
     Mike Micallef: pages xv, 12–13, 26, 52–53, 64–65, and
        96–97
     Leo Wesson: page xix

13 12 11 10 9 8 7 6 5 4
First Edition

To the Reata family, our guests and employees,
all of whom have supported us since we opened
the original Reata in Alpine, through the
tornado and all its aftermath. For yesterday, today,
and tomorrow—each of us would be a lone rider
without a horse if not for each of you.

CONTENTS

INTRODUCTION

When you roll into a new town and step out of your pickup to stretch your legs, you might look to the east and then to the west, but what if nowhere in sight can you spy a promising place to eat? Perhaps you settle for the local greasy spoon, or maybe you climb back in your rig and head on down the highway to the next town. Not my dad. He had just bought the ranch of his dreams in the Davis Mountains of West Texas, and as he saw it, there was only one thing missing. With no great restaurant in Alpine, he identified a business opportunity. But I'm getting seriously ahead of myself.

In the spirit of that wonderful old bumper sticker, my dad wasn't born in Texas but he got here as quick as he could. No, let me take that back. I believe that in some profound way, my father, Al Micallef, was *born* to be a Texan. When he was a boy, he read books about Texas and saw movies about Texas—many of them the cowboy-and-Indian shoot-em-ups that were standard issue for an American male growing up in the 1940s. He even curled up at night beside an old crystal radio, listening to "border-blaster" radio broadcasts from just across the Rio Grande River, the border between Texas and Mexico. Cowboys and Indians, sheriffs and outlaws, pirate broadcasters, and wildcat oilmen—these weren't just characters in stories to my dad as a child in Detroit, of all the unlikely places. In time, they were my dad. It was his destiny to become a Texan.

This book, about the glorious cuisine of the Lone Star State, is also the story of one American family who did, on the giant canvas that is Texas, what American families have always done: sought to make life a little better by taking risks and working hard. Today, our family is most visible in its Reata restaurants, the original in the tiny West Texas town of Alpine, and its much larger sibling in the increasingly sophisticated "cow-town" of Fort Worth.

Long before Texas meant gushing oil, JR Ewing, or the Dallas Cowboys, it meant steers on the open range. And it took rugged men unafraid of huge risks to take on Mother Nature and just about everybody else to raise cattle. This history has nurtured an attitude held by many Texans of entrepreneurship, those individuals seeing new opportunities and not afraid to bet the farm—or the ranch—on their next great idea. My father has that entrepreneurial DNA, with a dozen or more other enterprises in which he saw some beckoning opportunity. Truth is, Al Micallef never did anything halfway—he still doesn't. His life in Texas, and by association all our family's lives here, began with that most classic of Texas dreams: the cattle ranch.

This spirit *is* Texas to us, and it's Texas to millions of others today who have many colors of skin, who follow many faith traditions, who speak many languages. Together, I think I can say, we all want the same thing from this book you're holding in your hands—for you to come to know and love our Texas and her traditions just the way we do.

GONE TO TEXAS

Even for those of us who arrived much later, the words "Gone to Texas" have had special meaning since the early 1830s. It was in those years, when today's state was Mexican territory remaining from Spain's colonial empire, that the call for new settlers was answered all over the young country known as America. History tells us that folks simply packed up their houses and businesses, pointed their wagons west, and left behind only a hand-lettered sign over the door or nailed to the front gate: "Gone to Texas." That was all it said. It said a mouthful.

And it still does.

By the mid-1970s, had those settlers managed to stick around, they surely wouldn't have recognized the place. Beginning with momentous discoveries in the early twentieth century, Texas had become an oil and gas empire with considerable affluence and many jobs to spread around. High technology, such as it was back then, had come to Texas with NASA under Lyndon Johnson's space program and dug in as Texas Instruments and a few other early "computer" companies. No one knew it yet, but the business forces that would one day make Austin a technology powerhouse were beginning to transform Texas from within. So of course, my dad had to go and get all revved up not about oil and gas, not about calculators or computers, but about good, old-fashioned Texas cattle.

By 1975, shortly before the birth that would make me a native Texan, my father moved his family from Detroit to Fort Worth. As a business prodigy, he had risen to the upper management of a manufacturing firm at the age of twenty-four and decided, in hopes of becoming a cattle rancher too, that the company should essentially

post their own "Gone to Texas" sign. Before long, the manufacturing company had a new home and the Micallef family had embarked on a series of successful cattle ventures in the Fort Worth area. Our first ranch, on the Clear Fork of the Trinity River, took on the name CF. In a state that understood the value of branding *cattle* long before Madison Avenue made branding an all-encompassing concept, the CF Ranch was born.

As we discovered over the years, while our family grew with the arrival of my two sisters, Amanda and Sarah, so did Dad's ambition. Ranching on the green prairies of northeast Texas was one thing. Ranching on the dry, brown, and gray volcanic rock of West Texas was something else entirely. Still, my parents had visited friends in this area and soon found themselves thinking about another big gamble.

In 1992, they signed papers to purchase what became our headquarters ranch north of Alpine, in the heart of the majestic Davis Mountains. Over time Dad added other ranches south of Alpine, between Van Horn and Sierra Blanca, and in northeastern New Mexico.

Cattle ranching was very lucrative in the past, but today you can't pay for a ranch by just raising cattle. At one time, we had more than 150,000 acres, and in fact I remember one of my sisters asking Dad if he intended to buy all the land in Texas. "No, just everything that borders mine," he said with his trademark Al Micallef grin. Today, that number is reduced to some degree, much of it used for our cattle but some devoted to polo ponies and now to thoroughbreds. To share the beauty and splendor of the area, we've introduced some of the South Ranch to a residential development—large 20- to 30-acre spreads that we lease back to graze our cattle.

Ranching has been very good to my family, but there also hasn't been a single day that we, my dad in particular, haven't worked to do our jobs better. Today ranching is a business like any other, except that we get to work in the outdoors and see things people from cities can only dream of. The Ranch Management School at Texas Christian University began in 1956 and teaches students the day-to-day management of a working ranch, but it also instills a work ethic and attitude that you have to adapt to a constantly changing environment—or perish. I graduated with a Certificate in Ranch Management from TCU in 1997 and a BBA/Finance in 1999.

My father and I have searched out other activities we can do on the ranch with minimal impact to the land, our most valuable asset. Hunting is an important source of income for ranches these days, and in some places it has exceeded cattle revenues. Our ranch has been a popular location for shooting print ads, movies, TV shows, and music videos: *The Good Old Boys, Streets of Laredo, Dead Man's Walk, Rough Riders, Dancer Texas, Grand*

Champion, Cowboy U, and a Brooks & Dunn video, *A Man This Lonely,* just to name a few.

Even if you didn't already know what this book is about, you might see where this is all leading: managing Mother Nature to harvest one of its most popular foods, carefully balancing cost with revenue to make a fair profit, embracing the hospitality and entertainment industries almost as though they're the same—and of course doing what many do for romance or fun, but doing it seriously for a living. Still, to hear my father tell it, he didn't open the original Reata for any of these reasons. He propelled his family into the restaurant business because he kept turning up in Alpine and couldn't find anything good to eat.

THE ORIGINAL REATA

Over the years, talking with customers in both our Alpine and Fort Worth locations, I've been struck by how many non-Texans (and even some Texans) are surprised by the diversity of our "cowboy cuisine." In a way, though, this makes perfect sense—as many are even more surprised by the diversity of our cowboys.

Thanks to Hollywood, just about everybody thinks they know what a Texas cowboy is: how he dresses, how he talks, even how he moves and thinks. Yet few people understand how many centuries and how many ethnic groups fed into that single Hollywood stereotype. Few of the early Texas cowboys, for instance, spoke with that familiar "howdy pardner" Texas twang—because they were busy speaking *Spanish*. That explains why, going back even before the Republic of Texas was founded in 1836, a majority of our most beloved foods bore and still bear the signatures of the Spanish and Mexican empires. Furthermore, many of our cowboys didn't have deep, red-tinged suntans—because they happened to be African Americans, either former slaves or members of an elite cavalry force known as the Buffalo Soldiers. Texas, you understand, both had and was its own Ellis Island. Its very beginnings cried out for the bravest settlers, and/or the ones with the least to lose—the best, you might say, if not always the brightest. We even had our own port, Galveston, through which tens of thousands of immigrants poured from places like Sicily and Bohemia, even from Japan and China. Our Sicilians tended to become farmers and migrated to the rich-soiled southeast, while Germans, Czechs, and other middle Europeans congregated in the rockier Hill Country, their talents as butchers giving America the beginnings of Texas barbecue. Hispanic Texans always tended to live in the places they felt most comfortable, meaning the Rio Grande Valley that stretched from the Gulf of Mexico all the way west to the settlement known as El Paso del Norte (or El Paso for short).

Before the Republic, during our independence, and finally as America's 28th state, there were no hard-and-fast borders between these ethnic groups. They mixed and mingled, of necessity mostly but sometimes by choice, doing business, protecting themselves from frontier threats, and marrying each other's daughters. Honestly, while some people think they know what a Texas meal should taste like, almost *any* meal can be a Texas meal. And that's part of what we Texans are most proud of.

My dad, still hungry, quickly found that Holy Trinity of the restaurant business in Alpine—location, location, location—establishing his eatery downtown in an old adobe house from the 1880s. He was inspired in every decision, it seems, by the fact that décor and cuisine came together in a setting authentically and historically associated with the people whose memory we were honoring. We worked with a decorator here and there, with a trained chef here and there too, but the vision of Reata was always my father's. What he wanted, and what we want now, is a damn good place to eat. We believe the

best way to achieve that is with a great attitude and an innovative celebration of Texas culinary history—a menu that's free of the deprivation that was typical for cowboy cooks yet that would build every single flavor from something Texans have loved for generations.

The name Dad chose for our family's restaurant was something of a natural, yet definitely a stroke of genius as well. The word *reata* is Spanish for "rope," and there couldn't be a more basic, essential tool for the cowboy than that. You simply can't go about ranchin' without one. Yet the name, from the beginning, drew upon the mystique of another, less workaday West Texas icon. Reata had been the name of the ranch, the homestead—the Tara, if you will—in the myth-spinning 1956 film *Giant*, based on the Edna Ferber novel. The movie starred Elizabeth Taylor, Rock Hudson, and James Dean and was released only two weeks before Dean was killed in a car wreck. Filmed about 20 miles away from

Alpine in the vicinity of Marfa, *Giant* set the tone for fictional treatments of Texas ranch families for decades to come. In other words, with the name my father chose for our restaurant, we were drawing together everything that was real about Texas ranch life and everything that was legendary as well.

Even with our strong grounding in Texas food, we still had to grapple with what would be one of our biggest challenges: the importance of our chef. On the one hand, we knew what we wanted to see and taste on each plate—and that meant nothing frou-frou, nothing wimpy, nothing out of character here in Texas. But we also launched the first Reata at the dawn of the Era of the Superstar Chef, when the guys who used to simply make our meals would evolve into guys who would make millions, front name-sake restaurants in Las Vegas, and entertain us on the Food Network. Truth is, we worked with a string of talented chefs at Reata and they received national media attention, but we've made the decision that it's more important to concentrate on the customer and have all of our chefs in Reata's kitchen, creating your next meal and experience. Today, whenever people ask us about our chefs, we tell them instead about our family: about our long experience on a real Texas cattle ranch, about our profound under-standing of Texas people, Texas history, and our team at Reata. Dad has always said you have to stay close to your roots.

BRAVE NEW WORLD

If you think it ever gets easy in the restaurant business—even when you have one operation running smoothly—then you haven't heard about our efforts to bring Reata to Fort Worth. The city has embraced our food since day one, we are grateful to report; but a series of unlikely and even tragic events taught us the age-old truth that what doesn't destroy you makes you stronger.

Reata in tiny Alpine, Texas, was a huge hit. We had customers coming in from all over the state, people who never imagined they'd come all the way to Alpine *for a meal*. And they sat right down under the row of cowboy hats (hung on the wall by working cowboys) and dug in to the pleasures of our food with gusto. Thanks to my father's essential notions about what would work at Reata, as well as contributions from our gifted chefs, our menu had taken exciting shape. Over time we found a motto to suit our mission: **REATA: Legendary. Texas. Cuisine.**

For instance, we knew our customers would want a good steak; and of course, as cattle ranchers, we were more than happy to supply them with one. Yet the traditional American steakhouse fare of red meat with baked potatoes and creamed spinach wasn't good enough for Reata, not for what we had in mind. We served (and still serve, as one of our signature entrées) pan-seared pepper-crusted tenderloin with port wine sauce. Or for those wishing a surprise from farther south, we have carne asada topped with what some call the best cheese enchiladas any-where. I'm not sure where the idea of covering steak with enchiladas came from exactly, but after you try our rendition, you'll want to move there. Around these and other beef-centric favor-ites grew a ceaselessly creative swirl of starters, sides, and desserts. Personally, I don't eat any-thing I use for bait, but even some seafood was allowed in!

Our customers couldn't get enough of our tenderloin tamales with pecan mash, and even ventured to sample our calf fries with cream gravy—we've been told we're America's larg-est seller of calf fries, which must be some kind of honor. Those seeking lighter fare fell in love with our totally trans-Pecos wedge salad with pico vinaigrette and crumbled bleu cheese, while lunch crowds packed in for our club sandwich with hand-cut fries or our equally eye-popping BLT, made with peppered apple-smoked bacon.

No matter how stuffed they claimed they were after their entrée, nobody ever seemed to hit the door without indulging in a signature dessert like our chocolate chunk bread pudding tamale (yes, it comes wrapped in a corn husk!) or our country-goes-decadent West Texas pecan pie.

We took these and a host of other dishes to our brand-new venture on the 35th floor of the Bank One Tower in Fort Worth, invited there by a close family friend and Fort Worth banker Bob Semple after he visited Reata Alpine. We understood that Fort Worth, or Cowtown, to us locals for its romanticized past of stockyards, cattle drives, and gunfights always inspired by women, whiskey, or both, was a much bigger and, in many ways, more demanding city. Obviously, there would be more competition for diners on any given night than there'd be in a month or even a year in our little West Texas town. But we were confident of our cooking, of our hard-won philosophies of wine and service, and (within reason) of the praise we'd received from local, regional, and national media. And my dad kept us sane. Despite his passion for every venture he undertook, he insisted on solid business principles and careful growth. When people say that most new restaurants fail within the first year or two, I'm pretty sure some of them wouldn't fail if they had my dad to keep their heads on straight.

Yet even a straight head can't save you from fate. On March 28, 2000, as on any other evening in the Bank One Tower, all was ready for dinner and we had begun seating guests. In a matter of minutes, however, everything we knew and counted on changed forever.

A funnel cloud began to spin mightily, and the skies turned an ominous green. The emergency sirens began to wail, and at 6:20 P.M., a whopper of a tornado hit downtown Fort Worth right in the gut.

Described by a long-time local media professional as "the most strange and indiscriminate tornado ever seen," an F2 tornado struck the very heart of the city, shattering high-rise buildings and collapsing whole neighborhoods along a two-mile path.

The first deadly twister in Fort Worth's history killed four people and injured more than a hundred others. City officials closed large segments of downtown for days to make the area safe for pedestrians. Weeks later, experts assessed the damage to Fort Worth at more than $450 million.

The heart of the city looked like a war zone; our restaurant was torn to shreds. Our staff barely had enough time to get our guests and themselves to safety in the fire exit stairwell. The floor-to-ceiling windows blew out, furniture spun through the air, and even the heaviest pieces of kitchen equipment went airborne. There are wild security videotapes of all this, and every time I watch them for a few moments I am amazed by the miracle that no one in Reata was killed.

We spent much of that night making sure every single one of our staff and guests were safe and back in the arms of loved ones, and also securing what was left of the Fort Worth Reata as best we could. By the next day, we had decided to rebuild. After all, we had a following from all over the Dallas-Fort Worth metroplex who knew where to find us, and the many businesses that shared our high-rise would depend on us to be there as they sought normalcy in the face of extremely abnormal circumstances.

In forty-two days following the tornado, with then-Reata president Mike Evans at the helm, we poured more than $1 million into the Herculean task of rebuilding and reopening. We brought back 100 percent of the staff, feeling that was simply the right thing to do for those who had sacrificed so much. What's more amazing, even as they were helping us rebuild, we knew that many of them were also volunteering with the Red Cross and other relief organizations, reaching out to other tornado victims in our own building and beyond.

To the astonishment of all, Reata reopened for business on May 9, 2000, with its menu and staff intact. The tornado and its after effects created hardship for not only Reata but also an entire city. Reata quickly became an example of what could be accomplished in a short period of time when a team comes together. Nevertheless, in January of 2001 we were forced to close. We made the announcement, and three days later we served our last meal. And those three days were the busiest we had experienced to date. We were touched by how emotional our guests were, knowing that *their* Reata was closing. It was a nonstop party, with as many toasts to the future as there were reminiscences about the great times from the past.

THE BRIGHT ROAD AHEAD

Though I'm often told that clouds have silver linings, you might excuse me if I don't extend that axiom to funnel clouds. Still, there was a silver lining of sorts. As always, with Dad's style of hard-nosed business thinking, we realized something about what was lost in Fort Worth—and turned it into something *found*. We had a tremendously loyal family of employees, we had some terrific recipes, and we had a good-as-gold reputation with our customers. What we didn't have was a place for people to come visit us. Like a phoenix born from the ashes, Reata on the Road was born.

We'd done a little catering before, of course, as almost every restaurant ends up doing some from time to time. But we'd been too busy opening and running two restaurants 480 miles apart to give it our full attention. Now we could, and now we did. Utilizing a 3,000-square-foot catering

kitchen, we took an extreme leap of faith into the world of private and corporate catering, cooking classes, and full-scale event production. Like our Reata menu was and is, Reata on the Road was everything we expected—and then some.

It's hard for me to look back at those days without remembering a phrase Dad always says, "If you're not making dust, you're eating dust." We took on any challenge that presented itself. And after what we'd been through with the tornado, cooking or transporting food just about anywhere seemed, well, small potatoes. Catering really allows you to get close to your customers. It got us deeply involved in our community with events ranging from the Main Street Fort Worth Arts Festival to one of our most treasured relationships, the Fort Worth Stock Show and Rodeo.

Since 1896 there has been an annual livestock show in Fort Worth, and since 2002 Reata has operated a full-service restaurant at this event, Reata at the Rodeo. In the beginning, Reata had just one dining room that was decorated to have the look and feel of our first Fort Worth home on the 35th Floor of the Bank One building. With nothing more than a tent to cook in and a staff that exceeded expectations, we served all the same favorites from the Reata menu, including the pan-seared pepper-crusted tenderloin and the quail with jalapeño cheese grits, and our reservation book was always filled. In the years that followed, we added a second room trying to quell the demand, but our only problem was how to accommodate all of our customers. After the 2007 rodeo, we were asked to take over the Backstage Club, an area that has been operated as a private club since the 1950s and that over-looks the rodeo arena.

This was a huge undertaking. We remodeled the space, building a whole new restaurant just for those three weeks of the rodeo. We were thrilled by the demand for memberships, recognition that patrons supported the product we were offering. We had 386 memberships before we were forced to stop selling; we simply had no reservation times left. By the end of the rodeo we had an additional 225 folks on the waiting list for memberships for the coming year. Having Reata at the Rodeo and Reata at Backstage, totaling 400 seats, while still running our flagship restaurants sure shows what a team can really do. We strive to offer the finest dining experience found at any rodeo, or for that matter at any top-level sporting event in the country.

Everybody who's ever visited Forth Worth knows about Sundance Square, named after a man even more colorful than my dad, the notorious outlaw, the Sundance Kid, who rode with the equally infamous Butch Cassidy. It's the city's chief dining and entertainment district, a stylish swirl of restaurants, bars, nightclubs, and music venues in a remarkable historic setting. As an urban redevelopment project, Sundance Square had been spearheaded since the early 1980s by local businessman and philanthropist Edward P. Bass. By the time we entered the picture, Sundance had a huge space that was crying out to be something wonderful. Lately occupied by a nightclub called Caravan of Dreams, it was no less than 22,000 square feet of intriguing components that included a recording studio, a theater, two dance spaces, a rooftop cactus garden, and a geodesic glass dome. What a challenge this location would be, and what an incredible opportunity.

Whereas many restaurants are essentially composed of a single room with a uniform look, Reata at Sundance would be much, much more. We are grateful to designer Carla Curry for helping us understand and embrace the many different spaces we have. Each area would have its own special signature, and each would be unforgettable. The motif that connects all the dots, however, is, just as it had been with the first Reata in Alpine, my family's love of the Old West. Reata at Sundance today is filled with museum-quality antiques and historical artifacts and memorabilia that celebrate the American cowboy, an icon that has become deeply rooted in our country's collective imagination. Photos of Texas ranches are part of the Reata experience, as are the spectacular silver saddles used in past Rose Bowl Parades and the chaps worn by the late Dan Blocker (unforgettable as Hoss Cartwright on the beloved TV show *Bonanza*), who attended Sul Ross State University in Alpine.

With kitchens on three levels and a much larger staff, we've been able to expand our menu beyond the list offered in Alpine—in fact, we now use Fort Worth to develop new recipes to be served in both restaurants. Spotting an opportunity, we were able to build a number of private dining rooms, large and small, into Reata at Sundance. Today, private dining accounts for 30 percent or more of our business at certain times of the year. It's exciting for a restaurant to be chosen when there's so much competition for business meetings, wedding engagements and rehearsal dinners, anniversary and retirement parties, and just about every other occasion the people of Fort Worth can think of to celebrate. We are grateful they select all of us at Reata to celebrate right along with them.

Why does Reata continue to grow? Why are we more successful today than at any other time in the past? There isn't just one answer, but first and foremost, it is that we're a single team with a single goal: exceed the customer's expectations.

That experience begins when customers call to make their reservation, when they drop off their car with our valet, when they are greeted and seated by one of our hostesses, and when they are taken care of by our bartenders, servers, managers, chefs, and kitchen staff. Any breakdown in the system can result in the customer's experience not being perfect. And if that happens, we've failed. They say the devil is in the details, and we take the details very seriously. Details like calling a guest a day or two after their meal and asking about the service, the food, and the ambience goes a long way toward perfecting that guest's experience. So does having the valets place thank-you cards in the vehicles with my phone number and e-mail address so the customer can communicate with me personally.

I know, we're a restaurant, and I enjoy talking about food. We've always used the freshest ingredients possible to make the kind of dishes you wouldn't mind eating a couple days a week. Each recipe in this book carries interesting descriptions about exactly what we use, how we use it, and why we are so happy with the finished product. But that's about when you're dining at our restaurant, and I have an additional endorsement: You may think I'm crazy, but I have personally tested every recipe in my home kitchen with the same kitchen appliances you have in your home. The reason for doing this is when you reduce a recipe that is supposed to

feed hundreds to a serving size of six you have to make some adjustments, and that's just what we did so you would have a wonderful Reata experience with this cookbook. So relax, roll up your sleeves, have some fun, and enjoy the great food.

We have come full circle, you see. Beginning our restaurant journey as a real Texas ranching family, we came to realize that at Reata, in Alpine, Fort Worth, and anywhere we grow from here, every plate and every glass lives in the imagination of each individual customer. Like *Giant*, the movie that gave us our inspiration and our name, what we're living each day is life. But what we're serving, in our restaurants and in all the pages that follow, is something so much larger, something, well, something just— GIANT!

STARTERS

ALPINE NACHOS - 2
Great Guacamole
Crème Fraiche

BACON-WRAPPED SHRIMP WITH THREE-ONION
MARMALADE AND POLENTA STARS - 4
Three-Onion Marmalade
Polenta Stars

BRAISED BOAR RIBS WITH SPICY PEANUT
DIPPING SAUCE - 6
Spicy Peanut Dipping Sauce

CALF FRIES - 8

CATFISH CAKES WITH SWEET PICKLE TARTAR
SAUCE - 9
Sweet Pickle Tartar Sauce
Tartar Sauce

CEVICHE MARTINI - 10

CHILI-FIRED SHRIMP WITH COLD CUCUMBER
SLAW - 15
Cold Cucumber Slaw

"GIANT" ONION RINGS WITH
SERRANO KETCHUP - 16
Serrano Ketchup

SMOKED QUAIL WITH SWEET MOLASSES GLAZE
AND JALAPEÑO-CHEDDAR GRITS - 19
Sweet Molasses Glaze
Jalapeño-Cheddar Grits

TENDERLOIN CARPACCIO WITH CILANTRO
HORSERADISH - 21
Cilantro Horseradish

TENDERLOIN TAMALES WITH PECAN MASH AND
SUN-DRIED TOMATO CREAM - 22
Masa Filling
Tenderloin Filling
Pecan Mash
Sun-Dried Tomato Cream

FRIED CALAMARI WITH COWBOY COCKTAIL
SAUCE - 25
Cowboy Cocktail Sauce

VENISON QUESADILLAS - 26

ALPINE NACHOS

Our homemade Pico de Gallo and Great Guacamole are the secrets to these best-selling nachos from our original West Texas restaurant. We think this is a great way to use up those tasty black or pinto beans left over from our Ranch-Style Beans recipe.

6   ounces tortilla chips (about half of a large bag)
2   cups Monterey Jack cheese, shredded
1   cup black beans, or pinto (rinsed and drained, if using canned)
2   grilled chicken breasts, cubed
1/2   cup Pico de Gallo (page 55)
1/3   cup Crème Fraiche, or sour cream
1/2   cup Great Guacamole

Preheat the oven to 300 degrees F. Create a mountain of tortilla chips on a large oven-safe platter. Sprinkle the shredded cheese over the chips and place in the oven. When the cheese melts and begins to bubble, and the edges of the chips begin to toast, remove from the oven. Evenly spread the beans and cubed chicken over the warm nachos. Pile Pico de Gallo in the center of the dressed nachos. Finish with a drizzle of the Crème Fraiche and a generous portion of Great Guacamole.

Great Guacamole

MAKES ABOUT 4 CUPS, DEPENDING ON THE SIZE OF THE AVOCADOS

4   ripe avocados
1   cup red onion, minced
1   cup roma tomato, diced
4   teaspoons lime juice
1   bunch cilantro, stemmed and chopped
1½   tablespoons kosher salt, or to taste

Cut each avocado in half. Use a sharp knife to strike the pit and imbed the blade. Twist the knife slightly to remove the pit, and discard. Score the avocado flesh while it is in the skin. With a spoon, gently scoop the diced flesh into a bowl. Repeat with the remaining avocados. Add the minced onions and diced tomatoes, and mix. Add the lime juice and salt, and mix. Add the cilantro, and mix well. Serve immediately.

Crème Fraiche

MAKES 1½ CUPS

3/4   cup sour cream
3/4   cup buttermilk
     Kosher salt
     Freshly ground black pepper

Combine all the ingredients in a bowl, whisking until the mixture has the consistency of salad dressing. Season with salt and pepper.

BACON-WRAPPED SHRIMP
WITH THREE-ONION MARMALADE
AND POLENTA STARS

SERVES 4 TO 6

Lots of folks like these prawns as a side to their steak or atop a salad. Polenta can also be used as a side starch, but then we recommend throwing in a few fresh jalapeño peppers or maybe some adobo sauce to kick the flavor up a notch or two. Then, simply cook the polenta at 350 degrees F for about 10 minutes, or until it begins to brown on top and around the edges.

18 Bacon-Wrapped Shrimp
2 cups Three-Onion Marmalade
6 Polenta Stars
1/3 cup red bell pepper, diced
1/3 cup green onion, diced

Preheat the oven to 350 degrees F. Place the pre-baked polenta and pregrilled shrimp in a baking dish in the oven for 5 to 7 minutes. The dish is done when the bacon becomes crispy, the shrimp starts to bubble, and the polenta begins to brown on top and around the edges. Spread the Three-Onion Marmalade in the center of a large platter, or on individual appetizer plates. Place the cooked shrimp in the Three-Onion Marmalade. Offset with the Polenta Stars. Mix together the diced red pepper and green onion, and garnish each serving with a spoonful of the mixture.

Bacon-Wrapped Shrimp

We recommend finishing the prawns in the oven with the polenta, as detailed on page 4, rather than cooking them through at this stage. If you're not serving the prawns with the polenta, or if you're feeling lazy, you can cook them all the way through on the grill. The shrimp is done when the bacon becomes crispy and the prawns start to bubble.

18 (or about 1½ pounds, depending on size and weight) fresh jumbo shrimp, raw, peeled, deveined, and deheaded, but with tails on
18 thick slices (or about 1 pound) bacon

Wrap 1 slice of bacon around each shrimp. Grill over medium heat until the bacon begins to cook and the shrimp just starts to become opaque.

Three-Onion Marmalade

MAKES 2 CUPS

2 tablespoons oil, for sautéing
2 teaspoons garlic, minced
2 red onions, chopped
2 yellow onions, chopped
2 tablespoons balsamic vinegar
1 tablespoon brown sugar
  Kosher salt
  Freshly ground black pepper
1 green onion, thinly sliced, using all of the green portion

In a small skillet, sauté the garlic in the oil over medium heat. Add the red and yellow onions and sauté until the onions are wilted. Add all the remaining ingredients, except the green onions. Cook over medium heat for 30 minutes, stirring often. Add the chopped green onion, and simmer for an additional 10 minutes. Remove from the heat.

Polenta Stars

MAKES 12 STARS

1 tablespoon oil, for sautéing
1 green onion, thinly sliced
2 teaspoons shallots, peeled and minced
3 cups cold water
3 cups whole milk
1½ teaspoon dried thyme, crumbled
1 tablespoon unsalted butter
1 teaspoon kosher salt
½ teaspoon freshly ground black pepper
2 cups dry polenta, or finely ground yellow cornmeal
1 cup asiago cheese, grated

In a large, heavy saucepan, sauté the green onions and shallots in the oil over medium heat for about 3 minutes. Add the water, milk, thyme, butter, salt, and pepper. Bring to a boil, then reduce the heat to a simmer. Slowly add the polenta, whisking constantly to prevent lumps. Cook the polenta over low heat until it thickens, usually about 15 minutes, stirring constantly. Remove from the heat and stir in the grated asiago.

Butter a rimmed baking sheet. Spread the polenta evenly in the baking sheet, smoothing the top with a spoon or spatula. Cover the polenta with plastic wrap and refrigerate for at least 1 hour. When the polenta is completely cooled, cut into stars (or other shapes, as desired) using a greased cookie cutter.

BRAISED BOAR RIBS WITH
SPICY PEANUT DIPPING SAUCE

→← SERVES 6 TO 8 →←

Sure, boar is great because of its unique flavor, but you really can use any type of short rib for this dish. The only thing we insist on is that you plan ahead, as the very best way to make these ribs is to let them braise for 8 hours so the meat gets so tender it just falls off the bones. Okay, the real truth is, you could boil the ribs in a covered stewpot for about an hour and a half instead, but they won't be as tender. The Orange-Sesame Dressing also makes a delicious dipping sauce for these ribs.

3½ pounds boar ribs
1 cinnamon stick
2 garlic cloves, whole and peeled
2 dried bay leaves
1 tablespoon dried thyme
3 tablespoons black peppercorns
 Water
 Peanut oil, for frying

Preheat the oven to 225 degrees F. Place the ribs and all the other ingredients in a deep baking dish with a lid. Cover the ribs completely with water. Place the lid on top of the baking dish, or cover tightly with several layers of aluminum foil. The goal is to make a very tight seal like a pressure cooker, so the water doesn't evaporate during cooking. Braise in a warm oven for 8 hours. For a quicker version, you can prepare the ribs the same way in a large stewpot, and then let them simmer for about 90 minutes over low heat.

Remove from the oven or stewpot and let the ribs rest for about 15 minutes. Cut the ribs into 2-piece sections. Finish the ribs by deep-frying them in the peanut oil at 350 degrees F for about 2 minutes, or on a medium grill until lightly browned.

Spicy Peanut Dipping Sauce

MAKES ABOUT 4 CUPS

1 teaspoon oil, for sautéing
1 teaspoon red pepper flakes
3 cups heavy cream
1 cup creamy peanut butter

Sauté the red pepper flakes in the oil over low heat. Slowly add the heavy cream. Whisk in the peanut butter, a spoonful at a time, whisking constantly so it doesn't burn.

CALF FRIES

SERVES 4 TO 6

Some call these little nuggets Rocky Mountain Oysters, while other folks call 'em Cowboy Caviar. No matter what your brand, calf fries have been around as long as cowboys have been roping calves. We totally understand if it makes you a little uneasy to think about eating something that once made a young bull so proud—after all, not everyone is a *vaquero*. Our supplier says we're the largest buyer of this Western delicacy in the whole United States. If you're inclined to dip, our Cracked-Pepper Cream Gravy is a great accompaniment.

20 calf fries, cleaned of the membrane (you can ask
      your butcher to do this for you)
    Egg Wash (page 140)
1¹/₂ cups Reata Flour Spice (page 138)
    Peanut oil, for frying
1 cup Cracked-Pepper Cream Gravy (page 83)

Dip each calf fry in the Egg Wash, then toss in the Reata Flour Spice to get an even coating. In a cast-iron skillet or deep fryer, heat the oil to

about 350 degrees F. Cook the calf fries, rolling them frequently, until they're golden brown all over, usually about 3 to 5 minutes, depending on your frying apparatus.

Drain the cooked calf fries on paper towels. They're best when served immediately, but you can reserve them in a baking dish in a warm oven. Serve with Cracked-Pepper Cream Gravy.

CATFISH CAKES WITH
SWEET PICKLE TARTAR SAUCE

Fishing for cats is a favorite pastime in Texas. Many a boy grew up with a rod in one hand and a fork in the other. City slickers might prefer to use crab for these cakes, and that's just fine with us. Just don't tell my dad, as he's pretty darn partial to catfish. It goes without saying that pickle preference is completely personal, so we've offered both Sweet Pickle Tartar and plain Tartar Sauce. One uses the Reata Pickles, but the other can be made with the pickle of your choice—and both are perfect companions with any fried fish.

1   pound fresh catfish fillets
      Water
4   teaspoons oil, for sautéing
2   tablespoons yellow onion, finely chopped
2   tablespoons green bell pepper, finely chopped
2   eggs, beaten
4   teaspoons Old Bay Seasoning
1/2   cup mayonnaise
2   teaspoons Dijon mustard
1   cup dried bread crumbs
2   teaspoons lime juice
4   teaspoons Reata Grill Spice (page 138)
2   teaspoons Tabasco sauce
2   teaspoons dried basil, crumbled
      Peanut oil, for frying
2   cups all-purpose flour

In a large pot of boiling water, poach the catfish for about 15 to 20 minutes, or until the fish begin to flake with a fork. Drain the poached fish in a colander, and place on a baking sheet to cool. In a large skillet, sauté the onions and peppers in the sautéing oil for about 5 minutes, or until the vegetables are soft, and set aside. When the catfish are cool enough to handle, crumble by hand into a large bowl. Add the beaten eggs, cooked onions, and peppers. Add the remaining ingredients and mix well to create a slightly wet, cake-like consistency that holds its shape.

Form the mixture into 6 to 10 round cakes of equal size, place on a baking sheet, and reserve until ready to fry. In a cast-iron skillet or deep fryer, heat the frying oil to about 350 degrees F. Just before frying, thoroughly dust each catfish cake with flour. Fry the cakes, turning frequently, until they're golden brown all over, usually about 3 to 4 minutes, depending on your frying apparatus. Drain the cooked catfish cakes on paper towels. Serve immediately, which is how they're best, or reserve them in a baking dish in a warm oven. Serve with Sweet Pickle Tartar Sauce.

Sweet Pickle Tartar Sauce

MAKES ABOUT 2 1/2 CUPS

1   cup Reata Pickles (page 140), diced
1/2   yellow onion, chopped
3/4   cup mayonnaise
1/4   cup sugar
1   bunch cilantro, stemmed and roughly chopped
      Kosher salt
      Freshly ground black pepper

Combine all the ingredients in a bowl. Cover and chill overnight to allow the flavors to blend thoroughly.

continued

Tartar Sauce

MAKES ABOUT 1½ CUPS

- 1 cup mayonnaise
- 1 teaspoon Dijon mustard
- 2 scallions, finely chopped
- 1 garlic clove, minced
- 1 shallot, finely chopped
- 1 tablespoon capers, drained and finely chopped
- 2 tablespoons dill pickles, diced
- ⅛ teaspoon cayenne pepper
- 1 tablespoon fresh parsley, finely chopped
- ½ teaspoon fresh tarragon, finely chopped
  Juice of 1 lemon
  Kosher salt

Combine all the ingredients in a bowl and stir well to thoroughly combine. Add the lemon juice and stir. Season with salt. Cover and chill overnight to allow the flavors to blend thoroughly.

CEVICHE MARTINI

→ SERVES 6 ←

Serving ceviche in a martini glass has a way of making you feel like you're eating something really "bad," when you're actually eating something that's healthy. While we've called for shrimp, ceviche can be made with any other raw white fish cut into bite-sized chunks. Just remember, the fresher the fish, the better the ceviche! Ceviche "cooks" by marinating in the lime juice. You'll know the fish is ready when the acid from the juice turns the flesh firm and opaque, just as if it had been cooked with heat. If you serve the ceviche with our Tortilla Crisps, just cut the tortillas a little wider before frying so you have more chip to dip.

- 1½ pounds fresh shrimp, raw, peeled, deveined, deheaded, and chopped
  Juice of 12 limes
- 5 teaspoons kosher salt, or to taste
- 1 teaspoon freshly ground black pepper, or to taste
- 4 roma tomatoes, diced
- 3 shallots, diced
- 3 green onions, roughly sliced
- 3 jalapeño peppers, seeded and minced
- 3 bunches cilantro, stemmed and roughly chopped
  Tortilla Crisps (page 30), or tortilla chips of your choice

In a small mixing bowl, squeeze the lime over the chopped shrimp. Season with salt and pepper. Add the tomatoes, shallots, green onions, jalapeños, and cilantro. Mix well until all the ingredients are thoroughly combined. Chill in a covered container in the refrigerator for about 6 hours. Serve with Tortilla Crisps or chips of your choice. This dish is also delicious all by itself or atop a fresh green salad with extra Pico de Gallo or our Fresh Guacamole on the side.

CHILI-FIRED SHRIMP WITH COLD CUCUMBER SLAW

The spiciness of the shrimp gets toned down by the cool, crisp flavors of the slaw, but if you're brave, then gobble the shrimp all on its own. You can always add some rice to cut the heat and serve as an entrée. The Cold Cucumber Slaw also makes a refreshing cool summertime side for grilled fish or chicken, or is excellent when combined with fresh baby greens to give a simple salad a little extra crunch.

Chili-Fired Shrimp

- 1/4 cup oil, for sautéing
- 18 (or about 1 1/2 pounds, depending on the size and weight) fresh jumbo shrimp, raw, peeled, deveined, deheaded, and butterflied, but with tails on
- 1/4 cup dried ancho chile peppers, slivered
- 2 cups raw peanut halves
- 1/2 cup sesame oil
- 1/4 cup soy sauce
- 1 cup Sweet Molasses Glaze (page 19)
- 30 to 40 green grapes
- 1 1/2 tablespoons Tabasco sauce
- 1 1/2 red pepper flakes, crushed
- 2 tablespoons unsalted butter
  Kosher salt
  Freshly ground black pepper

In a large skillet, heat the sautéing oil over medium-high heat. Sauté the shrimp for about 3 to 5 minutes, or until the shrimp becomes more opaque than clear. Add the anchos and the peanuts, and cook for about 3 more minutes, stirring occasionally. Add the sesame oil, soy sauce, 3/4 cup Sweet Molasses Glaze, grapes, Tabasco sauce, and red pepper flakes, and mix well.

When the mixture comes to a boil, add the butter and stir until it is completely melted. Season with salt and pepper. Serve immediately over a bed of chilled Cold Cucumber Slaw, and drizzle with the remaining 1/4 cup of Sweet Molasses Glaze.

Cold Cucumber Slaw

MAKES ABOUT 4 CUPS

- 4 cucumbers, peeled, seeded, and julienned
- 2 yellow onions, julienned
- 4 green onions, roughly chopped
- 1/4 cup white wine vinegar
- 1/4 cup water
- 1/4 cup canola oil
- 1 tablespoon sugar
  Kosher salt
  Freshly ground black pepper

Combine all the ingredients in a small bowl, and mix well. Season with salt and pepper. Cover and chill for at least 2 hours before serving with the Chili-Fired Shrimp.

"GIANT" ONION RINGS
WITH SERRANO KETCHUP

The bigger the onions the better! Our favorite kind is the Texas 1015, which is usually bigger than a baseball. Most 1015s are grown around Pecos, which interestingly enough was home to the world's first rodeo on July 4, 1883. Pecos grows onions so big you can use the rings to make a bowl for Calf Fries or serve 'em atop a salad or steak. Our spicy ketchup mimics the flavor of Serrano pepper, even though it doesn't have one speck of Serrano in it. This particular chili originates in Mexico and is so hot your mouth could catch fire. But don't let that scare you away from the Serrano Ketchup. We promise we've tamed it down just a hair.

6   large yellow onions, sliced into 1/2-inch rings
    Egg Wash (page 140)
3   cups Reata Flour Spice (page 138)
    Peanut oil, for frying

Dredge the onion rings in the Egg Wash, then liberally coat in the Reata Flour Spice. Repeat the Egg Wash/Flour Spice coating procedure once more on each slice of onion, so each ring is generously coated twice. In a cast-iron skillet or deep fryer, heat the oil to about 350 degrees F. Cook the onions, stirring frequently, until they're golden brown all over, usually about 4 minutes total, depending on your frying apparatus.

Drain the cooked onion rings on paper towels. Serve immediately, which is how they're best, or reserve them in a baking dish in a warm oven. Serve with Serrano Ketchup.

Serrano Ketchup

MAKES ABOUT 2 CUPS

1 1/2   cups ketchup
1 1/2   teaspoons Tabasco sauce
1 1/2   teaspoons Worcestershire sauce
1 1/2   teaspoons honey

Combine all the ingredients in a mixing bowl, and whisk thoroughly. Serve as a dipping sauce with the "Giant" Onion Rings.

SMOKED QUAIL WITH SWEET MOLASSES GLAZE AND JALAPEÑO-CHEDDAR GRITS

→→ SERVES 6 →→

Texas men and some Texas gals are hard to find in the city come the last weekend in February, because that's when quail season ends. Engaged in "the classic gentleman's sport," quail hunters are fanatics who spend huge amounts of money on improving habitat so they can hunt these birds without causing harmful environmental impact. Here's a great way to prepare quail, whether store bought or taken in the field. We really prefer smoking to give substantial flavor throughout the meat, but you can certainly choose to grill instead if you're short on time. Simply place the coated quail on a medium-high grill for about 10 minutes total, turning once, and skip the frying.

2 teaspoons Reata Grill Spice (page 138)
2 tablespoons canola oil
1/4 tablespoon fresh garlic, minced
6 quails, semi-boneless
   Peanut oil, for frying
3 cups Jalapeño-Cheddar Grits
1 cup Sweet Molasses Glaze
6 green onions, sliced in half, with the tops cut to 2 inches

Heat the smoker to about 250 degrees F. Place the Grill Spice, canola oil, and garlic in a large bowl and mix well. Dredge each quail in the mixture, coating thinly but thoroughly. Place the coated quail in the smoker for about 1 hour. Remove the quail and set aside to cool. When the quail are cool enough to handle, cut each bird in half lengthwise. Preheat the oven to 250 degrees F.

In a cast-iron skillet or deep fryer, heat the frying oil to about 350 degrees F. Fry each quail until it is hot throughout. This won't take long, about 2 to 3 minutes total, depending on your frying apparatus. Reserve the prepared quail in a baking dish in a warm oven until you're ready to serve them. Arrange the quail so that each half crosses the other on a bed of the Jalapeño-Cheddar Grits,

using about 1/2 cup of grits per serving. Drizzle the quail and the grits with Sweet Molasses Glaze. Garnish each serving with 2 green onion strips.

Sweet Molasses Glaze

MAKES 1 CUP

This glaze is easiest to drizzle when it's warm, though you certainly can reserve some for other uses as it tastes good on just about everything! It's excellent with almost any type of meat; just be sure and heat it up a little so it gets a bit runny before you drizzle, dollop, or smother.

1/4 cup Karo dark corn syrup
1/4 cup ketchup
1/4 cup brown sugar
1/4 cup apple cider vinegar

Combine all the ingredients in a large stockpot and cook over medium-high heat. Reduce the liquid until it becomes thick enough to coat the back of a spoon. Remove from the heat and strain through a fine mesh strainer.

continued

Jalapeño-Cheddar Grits

SERVES 6 TO 8

One of our most requested recipes in the history of the restaurant, these grits are so tasty, smooth, and aromatic that some customers have said they want to bathe in them! In fact, my sister Amanda has been known to put up a fight when someone dares to take a bite or two out of hers. We serve them as a side with just about everything on our menu. Some folks even take 'em home and heat 'em up for breakfast.

- 3 cups water
- 3 cups heavy cream
- 2 jalapeño peppers, seeded and minced
- 1 tablespoon kosher salt, or to taste
- 1 teaspoon freshly ground black pepper, or to taste
- 2½ cups dry grits
- 4 tablespoons unsalted butter
- 2 cups sharp cheddar cheese, grated

Combine the water, cream, jalapeños, salt, and pepper in a large saucepan and cook over high heat until the liquid reaches a rapid boil. At the boiling point, slowly whisk in the grits, stirring constantly to avoid lumps. Lower the heat to medium and continue to stir. Stirring frequently, cook until the grits are soft and creamy, usually about 30 to 40 minutes. Remove from the heat and add the butter and grated cheese. Season with more salt and pepper, if needed. Let cool slightly before serving so the grits can be mounded easily. They should be the consistency of mashed potatoes.

TENDERLOIN CARPACCIO WITH CILANTRO HORSERADISH

＊—＊ SERVES 6 *＊—＊*

Carpaccio is raw beef filet sliced into very thin shavings. Prepare it the night before you plan to serve it and slice right before the meal. The Cilantro Horseradish is also excellent with either version of our Prime Rib.

2 (6-ounce) beef tenderloin filets
Pinch of kosher salt
Pinch of freshly ground black pepper

Preheat a large, heavy skillet over high heat. Season both sides of each filet with salt and pepper. When the skillet is piping hot, sear each filet for a mere 30 seconds (yes, seconds!) on each side. Tightly wrap the seared tenderloins in plastic and freeze overnight. Remove from the freezer. Using a meat slicer or mandolin, slice the frozen beef into paper-thin shavings. Top each shaving with a small dollop of Cilantro Horseradish.

Cilantro Horseradish

MAKES 2 CUPS

2 cups mayonnaise
2 tablespoons fresh horseradish, grated
½ bunch cilantro, finely chopped
Juice of 1 lime
Kosher salt
Freshly ground black pepper

Combine all the ingredients in a bowl and whisk thoroughly. Serve with the Tenderloin Carpaccio.

TENDERLOIN TAMALES WITH PECAN MASH AND SUN-DRIED TOMATO CREAM

They say everything's bigger in Texas. Well, it takes two husks to wrap around the five ounces of filling we stuff these tamales with. They're so good, we sell more than 8,000 of them every year at Fort Worth's Main Street Arts Festival.

Masa Filling

2½ cups masa
3 cups fresh corn (about 6 ears, off the cob)
1¼ cups lard, or vegetable shortening
1 cup Rich Chicken Broth (page 30)
1 bunch cilantro, coarsely chopped
1 tablespoon kosher salt
1 tablespoon paprika

Combine all the ingredients in a mixing bowl, and using an electric mixer, process until well blended. The masa mixture should be the consistency of wet mud. To test, drop a spoonful of the mixture into a glass of cold water; if it floats, you have just the right amount of lard. If it sinks, add a little more lard, 1 tablespoon at a time, mixing well after each addition. Reserve.

Tenderloin Filling

2 pounds ground tenderloin, or ground beef with at least 20% fat (don't go any leaner here—fat gives flavor!)
1 yellow onion, finely chopped
1 red bell pepper, finely chopped
5 jalapeño peppers, seeded and diced
4 garlic cloves, minced
2 tablespoons ground cumin
2 tablespoons kosher salt
1 tablespoon ground coriander

Combine all the ingredients in a large bowl and mix well. Cover and refrigerate.

Tamales

45 dried corn husks

Soak the corn husks in hot water until pliable, usually about 1 to 2 hours. On a clean, dry work surface, place 2 corn husks end-to-end with about a 2-inch overlap in the middle. Grease your fingers well with lard or butter. Place about 2 tablespoons of the masa filling in the center of each husk, spreading the filling to within about 2 inches of the husks' edges. Next, place a generous portion, about 3 tablespoons per tamale, of the tenderloin filling in the center of the masa. Tightly roll up the husks lengthwise around the filling, then fold or tie each end.

We like to take some of the extra soaked husks and cut them in ⅛-inch-wide strips to use for the ties. You'll need 2 ties per tamale, one for each end.

Place the tamales in a single layer on a steaming rack in a pot with a tight-fitting lid. You will probably need to cook these in 2 batches. Set the rack of tamales over about 1½ inches of boiling water. Cover the pot and let it steam for about 1 hour, adding water as needed to maintain the 1½ inches of liquid.

Slice an opening in the top of each tamale. To serve, place the tamales on a platter and top

continued

with about 1 tablespoon of the Pecan Mash and at least 1 tablespoon of the Sun-Dried Tomato Cream.

Pecan Mash

MAKES ABOUT 1½ CUPS

In Texas, we have no fear of turning tradition on its ear. Although we love the classic Italian pesto, we've parted with tradition and created our own unique version with pecans and cilantro. Just like its European cousin, our Pecan Mash still makes a great dipping sauce for bread. It's also excellent tossed with the Sun-Dried Tomato Cream on some al dente pasta. It wouldn't hurt a thing to throw in a leftover crushed tamale or two—you could call it Tamale Spaghetti.

- ¾ cup pecan pieces
- 2 garlic cloves, coarsely chopped
- 1 bunch cilantro, finely chopped
- ¾ cup asiago cheese, grated
- 1 to 2 jalapeño peppers, seeded and diced
- 1 to 1½ cups extra virgin olive oil
  Kosher salt

Combine the pecans, garlic, cilantro, cheese, jalapenos, and ¼ cup of the olive oil in a food processor. Pulse repeatedly to coarsely chop the pecans. With the machine running, slowly add the remaining olive oil, and process until all the oil is thoroughly incorporated. Season with salt. Cover and refrigerate.

Sun-Dried Tomato Cream

MAKES ABOUT 5 CUPS

- 1 tablespoon oil, for sautéing
- 2 garlic cloves, minced
- 4 tablespoons unsalted butter
- ½ cup rehydrated sun-dried tomatoes, puréed, or very finely chopped
- 1 quart heavy cream
- ½ cup parmesan cheese, grated
  Kosher salt
  Freshly ground black pepper

Heat the sautéing oil in a saucepan over medium-high heat. Add the garlic and sauté for about 2 minutes, until the garlic begins to brown. Add the butter and sun-dried tomatoes and cook for 1 to 2 minutes, stirring constantly. Lower the heat and slowly add the cream. Simmer for another 15 to 20 minutes, stirring constantly, until the liquid has been reduced by about 50 percent. Add the cheese and stir well. Season with salt and pepper. Remove from the heat and serve warm, or refrigerate until you're ready to reheat for future use.

FRIED CALAMARI WITH COWBOY COCKTAIL SAUCE

⟶ SERVES 6 ⟵

It's the dried jalapeño (or habanera) pepper spice that gives you that "just-kicked-with-a-spur" feeling when eating our Fried Calamari. The jalapeño spice is sometimes a little hard to find if you're not in rodeo country, but dried habanera can be found in most grocery stores. Combined with the Cowboy Cocktail Sauce, this squid is not for the faint of heart!

1   pound squid steak, cut into ½-inch strips (should yield 20 to 25 pieces)
     Egg Wash (page 140)
¾   cup Calamari Spice
     Peanut oil, for frying

Dredge each squid strip in the Egg Wash and then roll in the Calamari Spice until thoroughly coated. In a cast-iron skillet or deep fryer, heat the oil to about 350 degrees F. Fry the coated calamari strips, turning frequently, until they're golden brown all over, usually about 6 to 8 minutes total, depending on your frying apparatus. Drain the cooked calamari on paper towels. Serve immediately, which is how they're best, or reserve them in a baking dish in a warm oven. Serve with Cowboy Cocktail Sauce for dipping.

Calamari Flour Spice

MAKES ABOUT 1 CUP

¾   cup all-purpose flour
2½   tablespoons Reata Grill Spice (page 138)
1   teaspoon dried jalapeño spice, or ¼ teaspoon dried habanera spice (more if you like it screamin' hot!)

Combine all the ingredients in a large bowl.

Cowboy Cocktail Sauce

MAKES ABOUT 2 CUPS

1½   cups ketchup
2   teaspoons fresh horseradish, finely grated
     Juice of 1 lime
1   tablespoon fresh cilantro, finely chopped
½   teaspoon Tabasco sauce
     Kosher salt
     Freshly ground black pepper

Combine all the ingredients in a bowl and mix well. Season with salt and pepper. Serve as a dipping sauce with the Fried Calamari.

VENISON QUESADILLAS

↠ SERVES 1, BECAUSE THEY'RE MADE ONE AT A TIME,
BUT SIMPLY MULTIPLY THE INGREDIENTS BY THE NUMBER OF QUESADILLAS
YOU WISH TO MAKE SO YOU'LL HAVE PLENTY TO SHARE! ↞

Quesadillas are a great way to use any game meat. If you aren't a hunter—and aren't lucky enough to have one sharing his haul with you—just take the Sweet Molasses Glaze and drizzle it on top of a chicken or beef quesadilla for a taste that takes traditional Mexican to a whole new level.

½ tablespoon peanut oil, for frying (As the mixture reheats, it will spread and flatten even more.)
1 large flour tortilla
2 tablespoons mild cheddar cheese, shredded
2 tablespoons Monterey Jack cheese, shredded
1 yellow onion, diced
¼ bunch fresh cilantro, roughly chopped
Leftover venison, cooked and thinly sliced
1 tablespoon Sweet Molasses Glaze (page 19)
2 tablespoons Great Guacamole (page 2)

Heat the oil in a skillet over medium heat. Spread the shredded cheeses over the tortilla. Sprinkle the onion and chopped cilantro over the shredded cheeses. Next, add the layer of cooked venison on the dressed tortilla. Gently fold the tortilla and press down firmly, taking care that the filling doesn't escape. Place the folded tortilla in the hot, oiled skillet. Flip to the other side when the cheese "glues" the filling to the tortilla and the outside turns golden brown. Remove when both sides are lightly toasted. Cut into 3 triangles and drizzle with Sweet Molasses Glaze. Top with a generous dollop of Great Guacamole.

SOUPS

CLASSIC TORTILLA SOUP – 30
Rich Chicken Broth
Tortilla Crisps

FRED'S SPICY CHICKEN GUMBO – 32

HEARTY BEEF STEW – 33

JALAPENO-CILANTRO SOUP – 35

SUMMERTIME GAZPACHO – 36

VENISON CHILI – 37

CLASSIC TORTILLA SOUP

Our tortilla soup has been around the restaurant since the day we opened. If you're in a hurry and you just can't wait to make the Rich Chicken Broth, you can use a grilled chicken breast or pull the meat from a rotisserie chicken and use ready-made chicken broth. Heck, if you're in that much of a pinch, your favorite tortilla chips can also be used instead of deep-frying the tortillas for the Tortilla Crisps. But honestly, once you make this all the way through, we bet you'll never do it any other way.

Rich Chicken Broth

**MAKES ABOUT 2 QUARTS
(MAKE A BUNCH AND FREEZE SOME FOR LATER.)**

- 5 chicken legs and thighs
  Water
- 4 shallots, peeled
- 1 whole head garlic, peeled
- 2 carrots
- 1 tablespoon fresh black peppercorns
  Kosher salt
  Freshly ground black pepper

Place the chicken in a large, heavy stockpot with a lid. Add the water, shallots, garlic, carrots, and peppercorns. The liquid should just barely cover the chicken, so adjust the depth of the water, if needed. Heat over medium-high heat and bring the mixture to a boil. As the liquid begins to heat, skim off the foam that rises to the surface, and discard. When it begins to boil, lower the heat to a constant simmer. Continue skimming as needed. Cover the pot, leaving the lid slightly ajar, and continue cooking for 90 minutes.

Remove the pot from the heat, and leave the chicken in the broth for 30 minutes, until thoroughly cool. When the chicken is cool enough to handle, remove the skin and the bones and discard. Shred the remaining chicken, there should be about 3 cups, and reserve in a covered container that can be reheated at serving time.

Strain the remaining broth, there should be about 2 quarts, and return to a clean saucepan. Skim off any fat that has accumulated on the surface. Season with salt and pepper.

Tortilla Crisps

- 6 corn tortillas
  Peanut oil, for frying

Heat the oil in a cast-iron skillet or deep fryer to approximately 350 degrees F. Cut the tortillas into ¼-inch strips. Fry the strips for about 1 minute on each side, until they're crispy and lightly toasted.

Assembling the Soup

- 3 cups cooked, shredded chicken (reserved from the Rich Chicken Broth)
- 6 to 8 cups Rich Chicken Broth
- 1 to 2 limes, cut into generous wedges
- 2 to 3 jalapeño peppers, seeded and chopped
- 2 to 3 avocados, ripe but firm, cut into ½-inch cubes
- 1 cup Monterey Jack cheese, shredded
- ⅓ bunch fresh cilantro, chopped

Reheat the chicken and the broth separately, until the chicken is warm and the broth is hot.

continued

For each serving, place approximately ½ cup of the shredded chicken in each bowl. For each serving, top the chicken with 1 teaspoon of the chopped jalapeños, the juice from at least 1 lime wedge, 1 heaping tablespoon of the cubed avocados, and 2 heaping tablespoons of the shredded cheese. Finish with a generous helping of the crispy tortilla strips and a sprig of cilantro.

FRED'S SPICY CHICKEN GUMBO

—◆— SERVES 4 TO 6 —◆—

We just can't remember a time when Fred wasn't cooking in our kitchen. Fred's actually a lot like his gumbo—a little spicy, bold, robust, and full of heart! Unlike a lot of gumbo recipes, this one is made without okra. Fred uses an herb called gumbo file, made from the ground leaves of the sassafras tree. The herb essentially acts like powdered okra to help thicken the gumbo, without that gummy or stringy effect that okra sometimes has on a stew. Gumbo file can typically be found in the spice aisle at the grocery store.

2 cups extra virgin olive oil
2 cups all-purpose flour
1 red bell pepper, chopped
1 yellow onion, chopped
2 celery stalks, chopped
1 (12-ounce) can diced tomatoes
1 tablespoon dried thyme
1 tablespoon freshly ground black pepper
2 dried bay leaves
1 pound andouille sausage, diced
10 cups Rich Chicken Broth (page 30)
1 garlic clove, minced
1 tablespoon kosher salt
2 (8-ounce) chicken breasts, boneless, skinless and cut into ½-inch cubes
1 tablespoon gumbo file

In a large stockpot, heat the oil over medium heat. Slowly add the flour to make a roux, stirring with a wooden spoon or a whisk until the flour turns dark brown, about 6 to 10 minutes. Lower the heat and add all the remaining ingredients, except the chicken and gumbo file. Increase the heat and bring the mixture to a boil. Lower the heat to medium, and continue to cook until the gumbo is reduced by about 30 percent. Add the chicken and gumbo file. Continue cooking over medium-low heat for about 10 to 15 minutes, or until the chicken is fully cooked. The chicken is done when the meat is firm and white.

Be sure not to let the stew get too hot at this stage, or the gumbo file could turn stringy. Serve on its own or over rice for a satisfying main meal in a bowl.

HEARTY BEEF STEW

—✦— SERVES 8 TO 10 —✦—

A perfect dish to serve with Reata's Cornbread on a cold winter day. For those who like to hunt, venison or other game can easily be substituted for beef. You can make this even more filling by adding 2 cups of fresh potatoes with the other vegetables—just remember to cut them into ½-inch cubes and lightly boil them first.

1	cup extra virgin olive oil
1	cup all-purpose flour
1½	pounds stew meat, cubed into 1-inch squares
1	yellow onion, diced
1	celery stalk, diced
2	carrots, diced
2	garlic cloves, minced
1½	cups red wine
¼	cup tomato paste
1	(12-ounce) can diced tomatoes
2	tablespoons dried thyme
1	cup sliced mushrooms
2	dried bay leaves
3	cups frozen vegetables—mixture of corn, peas, and green beans (Fresh vegetables can certainly be used; just be sure to blanch, boil, or steam them lightly first, until just tender.)
12	cups water
¼	cup beef base
	Kosher salt
	Freshly ground black pepper

In a large stockpot, heat the olive oil over medium heat to approximately 325 degrees F. Add the stew meat and brown on all sides. Add the flour and stir well. Add the onions, celery, and carrots and lightly sauté. Add the minced garlic and stir well until all the ingredients are combined. Deglaze the stockpot with the red wine, combining the flavors of all that have cooked in the pot to this point. Add the tomato paste and diced tomatoes, and stir until all the ingredients are well combined. Add the remaining ingredients. Simmer over low heat for about 30 minutes, or until the vegetables are tender but not too soft.

JALAPEÑO-CILANTRO SOUP

— SERVES 6 —

This rich and creamy pepper bisque always seems to surprise our guests the first time they try it. The subtle flavors are as comforting as a warm wooly blanket on a soft downy bed—in fact, it's really hard to not curl up for a nap after you've had a bowl.

1/2 tablespoon unsalted butter

5 jalapeño peppers, seeded and minced

2 tablespoons garlic, minced

3/4 cup red onion, finely chopped

1 avocado, peeled and diced

4 roma tomatoes, diced

8 cups heavy cream (use the highest fat content available)

Kosher salt

Freshly ground black pepper

1 bunch cilantro, stemmed and chopped

Tortilla Crisps (page 30)

In a large stockpot, heat the butter over medium heat. Sauté the jalapeños, onions, and garlic for about 10 minutes, or until the onions are translucent and the peppers turn soft. Remove from the heat and add the avocado, tomatoes, and cream. Lower the heat, then return the pot to heat, stirring constantly so the cream doesn't separate. Slowly bring the soup back to a simmer, cooking to reduce by about 30 percent, stirring often to prevent scorching or sticking. Season with salt and pepper. Just before serving, add the cilantro, reserving about 1 teaspoon per serving for garnish. Sprinkle with the reserved chopped cilantro and Tortilla Crisps.

Roasted Tomato-Basil Soup

SERVES 6

Roasted tomatoes are quicker to make than you think, and they impart a really robust taste for this variation on a childhood favorite. Vegetable stock is preferred for the best flavor, but water can be used if you don't have any stock handy. Add a grilled cheese sandwich and presto—it's just like you're seven years old again.

8 tomatoes, whole for grilling, then diced when cool

4 tablespoons unsalted butter

2 celery stalks, diced

1 carrot, peeled and diced

1/2 yellow onion, diced

1 (6-ounce) can tomato paste

1/4 cup white wine

2 cups vegetable stock, or water

1 pint heavy cream

1 cup fresh basil, stemmed and roughly chopped

1/2 cup asiago cheese, shredded

Kosher salt

Freshly ground black pepper

Heat the grill to medium and roast the whole tomatoes. When the skins begin to look soft and start to separate from the tomato flesh, remove from the heat and set aside to cool. In a large heavy stockpot, melt the butter over medium-low heat and add the diced celery, carrots, and onion. Sauté the vegetables until the onions are soft, translucent, and beginning to brown. Dice the roasted tomatoes when they are cool to the touch. Add the diced tomatoes to the other sautéed vegetables. Add the tomato paste and white wine. Stir until thoroughly combined.

continued

Add the vegetable stock (or water) and bring the mixture to a simmer over low heat. Cover and let reduce by about 50 percent, checking occasionally to make sure the heat remains low and the mixture does not scorch. In a separate saucepan, combine the heavy cream with the chopped basil. Bring the cream-basil mixture to a simmer over low heat. Slowly add the warm basil cream to the tomato mixture and stir well. Let the mixture cool before placing in a food processor or blender. Purée the soup until smooth, and season with salt and pepper.

SUMMERTIME GAZPACHO

→ SERVES 6 →

Texas summers are so scorchin' hot, you almost never catch anyone eating hot soup from June to September. But a chilled gazpacho is a different story. This is an easy, cool, refreshing first course that makes a great introduction to grilled fish. It's also a surprising appetizer served in shot glasses at a backyard barbecue, or offered in martini glasses at a ladies' lunch.

6   roma tomatoes, diced
2   red onions, diced
2   cups fresh basil, finely chopped
3   celery stalks, diced
3   (6-ounce) cans tomato juice
1   teaspoon freshly ground black pepper
1   tablespoon kosher salt
1   tablespoon sugar
1   tablespoon Tabasco sauce
1   to 2 limes, cut into slim wedges

Combine all the ingredients in a mixing bowl. Cover and chill in the refrigerator for at least 2 hours before serving. Garnish each serving with a squeeze or two of lime.

VENISON CHILI

Where we come from, there's a chili cook-off almost every weekend somewhere in Texas. In fact, the Terlingua International Chili Championship is held every November, just south of our Alpine restaurant, where award-winning recipes are often kept under lock and key. We've even heard of some folks offering up their legendary recipes for collateral in a card game! We think chili's kinda like family—each individual ingredient (or person) is special in its own way, but it's about how they all come together that really counts. Feel free to play around with the types and amount of pepper spice so you can make this chili your own. You can also substitute buffalo or beef rib eye, boneless sirloin or chuck roast, or ground beef or turkey if it's off-season for venison.

4   pounds venison steak, cut into 1-inch cubes

3   tablespoons oil, for sautéing

2   yellow onions, diced

4   tablespoons fresh garlic, minced

4   tablespoons chili powder

3   tablespoons ground cumin

16   roma tomatoes, diced

2   bottles dark beer

1   cup Veal Stock (page 145, but if you don't have time to make the Veal Stock, blend ½ cup of chicken broth with ½ cup of beef broth)

½   cup masa

½   cup water

6   tablespoons dried oregano, crumbled

4   tablespoons kosher salt

1   tablespoon ground cayenne pepper

In a large, heavy stockpot, sauté the cubed venison in the oil until it is about halfway browned. Add the onions and garlic and continue to sauté until the onions become soft, translucent, and are beginning to brown. Add the chili powder, cumin, and tomatoes. Stir constantly over medium heat for 5 to 10 minutes. Add the beer and Veal Stock. Reduce the heat to low and simmer for 1 hour, stirring often. Add the masa to ½ cup water and dissolve thoroughly.

When the meat in the stockpot is tender and begins to shred, add the dissolved masa liquid. Add the oregano, salt, and cayenne. Simmer the chili for an additional 30 minutes over low heat. Remove from the heat and cover. Allow the chili to set for 2 hours before serving.

SALADS & DRESSINGS

ARGENTINE STEAK SALAD - 42

Bacon Balsamic Vinaigrette

AVOCADO CAESAR WITH GRILLED STEAK - 45

Avocado Caesar Dressing

FIELD GREENS WITH GOAT CHEESE AND SPICY PECANS - 46

Sherry Vinaigrette
Spicy Pecans

ALPINE SALAD BOWL - 48

Buttermilk Dressing

SOUTHWEST SALAD - 51

TEXAS WEDGE - 55

Pico Vinaigrette
Pico de Gallo

ARGENTINE STEAK SALAD

Texans may not think we have a lot in common with other places. In fact, we often refer to our state as a whole other country! But just like Texans, the beef-loving citizens of Argentina love their steak. One of my family's favorite restaurants is La Vaca Atada (translation: The Tied Cow) in Lobos, Argentina. The dressing of choice for this steak salad is Bacon Balsamic Vinaigrette, which is also excellent on fresh spinach. But we also highly recommend the Orange-Sesame Dressing on this salad.

1¼	pounds skirt steak, grilled, trimmed, and sliced
2	tablespoons Reata Grill Spice (page 138)
4	cups baby arugula
4	cups romaine, shredded
1½	cucumbers, thinly sliced
½	cup bleu cheese, crumbled
1	cup Bacon Balsamic Vinaigrette
2	tomatoes, sliced into wedges

Heat the grill to high. Season each side of the skirt steak with Reata Grill Spice. Grill the steak to medium-rare on each side. Remove from the heat, and allow to cool slightly before serving. Slice the steak to a thickness of about ¼ inch.

Toss the arugula and romaine in a large bowl. Top each serving with sliced cucumber and sliced steak. Drizzle each salad with the Bacon Balsamic Vinaigrette. Top with crumbled bleu cheese and tomato wedges.

Bacon Balsamic Vinaigrette

MAKES 2 CUPS

8	strips bacon, cooked crisp (set aside the drippings after bacon is cooked)
2	tablespoons flour
1	cup water
¾	cup balsamic vinegar
4	tablespoons sugar
2	teaspoons kosher salt
2	teaspoons freshly ground black pepper

In a cast-iron skillet over medium-high heat, fry the bacon until crisp. Remove from the skillet and place on paper towels to cool and dry. Lower the heat to medium-low and slowly whisk the flour into the warm bacon drippings until thoroughly dissolved. Add the water, balsamic vinegar, sugar, salt, and pepper, stirring constantly. Simmer the dressing over medium heat for about 10 minutes, or until it is reduced by about 50 percent. Let cool for 10 to 15 minutes before serving, allowing the dressing to thicken. Crumble the cooked bacon strips and add. Pour the dressing over the salad and toss well, and serve immediately.

AVOCADO CAESAR WITH GRILLED STEAK

We love fresh, ripe avocados so much that, if we had to, we might even spread them on cardboard. So it's no surprise we've given the traditional tangy Caesar a healthy dose of avocados. While most varieties add some dainty shrimp or tiny chicken strips, we add smoky flank steak with creamy avocado and a dressing that ain't afraid of anchovies, turning the kingly Caesar into a meal fit for a true roper.

  5 to 6 ounces flank steak, grilled, trimmed,
     and sliced
 ½ tablespoon Reata Grill Spice (page 138)
  3 cups romaine lettuce, chopped
 ¼ cup Avocado Caesar Dressing
 ½ cup Sourdough Croutons (page 130)
  1 to 2 tablespoons asiago cheese, grated
  2 tablespoons Sweet Molasses Glaze (page 19)

Heat the grill to high. Season both sides of the skirt steak with the Reata Grill Spice. Grill on both sides to a medium-rare. Remove the steak from the heat, and let cool slightly before serving. Slice to ¼-inch thickness.

Toss the romaine and the Avocado Caesar Dressing in a bowl and mix well. Place dressed lettuce on a plate and top with the Sourdough Croutons and asiago. Top each salad with warm, sliced steak. Drizzle Sweet Molasses Glaze over each serving.

Avocado Caesar Dressing

MAKES 4 CUPS

To make Avocado Caesar Dressing, simply add 1 peeled and chopped avocado and 2 tablespoons chopped fresh cilantro to 2 cups of the Caesar Dressing in a food processor or blender and combine on high.

  1 (2-ounce) can of anchovies, drained and minced
  3 cloves fresh garlic, peeled and minced
  1 egg yolk
  1 tablespoon Worcestershire sauce
  1 tablespoon freshly ground black pepper
  2 tablespoons dried ground mustard
 ¼ cup Dijon mustard
  2 tablespoons lime juice
  4 cups extra virgin olive oil
     Cold water, as needed
     Kosher salt
     Freshly ground black pepper

Place all the ingredients, except water and oil, in a blender or food processor and mix until combined well. Carefully open the blender or food processor, and, with the motor running, slowly drizzle in the oil in a steady stream, so the dressing emulsifies and thickens. If the dressing becomes too thick, thin it with water, 1 tablespoon at a time. Serve immediately, or refrigerate in an airtight container and shake vigorously just before serving.

FIELD GREENS WITH GOAT CHEESE AND SPICY PECANS

→ SERVES 1 ←

People love this as a first course, or sometimes topped with grilled chicken, Bacon Wrapped Shrimp, or even leftover tenderloin for a more substantial meal. The secret of the dressing is roasting the shallots for a mellower flavor, and the spicy pecans are so addictive we catch servers eating them in the kitchen by the handful!

2 cups mixed field greens
2 tablespoons goat cheese
3 cherry tomatoes, halved
¼ Granny Smith apple, thinly diced
2 tablespoons Spicy Pecans
2 tablespoons Sherry Vinaigrette

Toss the greens with the Sherry Vinaigrette dressing. Add 2 or 3 small dollops of goat cheese and the tomato halves around the edge of the salad. Top with a small handful of the diced apples and Spicy Pecans. Drizzle with the Sherry Vinaigrette.

Sherry Vinaigrette

MAKES 2 CUPS

3 tablespoons Roasted Shallots (page 132) or
   1 large shallot, minced
⅓ cup sherry wine vinegar
1 egg yolk
1 cup extra virgin olive oil
¼ teaspoon kosher salt
½ teaspoon freshly ground black pepper
1 tablespoon lemon juice
   Cold water

Place the shallots and vinegar in a blender and purée. Add the egg yolk and blend. Carefully open the blender, and, with the motor running, slowly drizzle in the oil in a steady stream so the dressing emulsifies and thickens. If the dressing becomes too thick, thin it with water, 1 tablespoon at a time. When dressing reaches a thick but pourable consistency, add the salt, pepper, and lemon juice and blend briefly. Serve immediately, or refrigerate in an airtight container and shake vigorously just before serving.

Spicy Pecans

1 tablespoon unsalted butter
½ pound pecan halves
⅓ cup brown sugar
1 tablespoon chili powder

Preheat the oven to 250 degrees F. Melt the butter in a small saucepan over low heat. Place the pecans in a mixing bowl, add the melted butter, and mix thoroughly. Add the brown sugar and chili powder, and mix until all the pecans are well coated. Spread evenly on a baking sheet and bake at 250 degrees F for about 45 minutes. Remove from the oven to let the pecans cool and dry. When the nuts are cool and crisp to the touch, place in an airtight container.

ALPINE SALAD BOWL

⟶ SERVES 1 ⟵

In Alpine, regulars have gone nuts for this twisted pasta salad that combines our unique Pecan Mash with toasted pumpkin seeds. Spiral or penne matters not, as long as you've got enough of our rich homemade Buttermilk Dressing to coat the pasta, you'll love this great combination of crisp lettuce, cool pasta, and nutty flavors.

$\frac{1}{2}$ cup fusili pasta, cooked and cooled
2 tablespoons Pecan Mash (page 24)
2 tablespoons pumpkin seeds, toasted
1 to 2 tablespoons asiago cheese, shredded
2 cups romaine lettuce, chopped
$\frac{1}{4}$ cup Buttermilk Dressing
1 chicken breast, grilled or breaded, and cubed
6 grape tomatoes, halved

Toss the pasta with the Pecan Mash, toasted pumpkin seeds, and asiago cheese in bowl. In a separate bowl, toss the romaine with Buttermilk Dressing. Place the pasta on serving plates. Add the dressed romaine to each serving. Top with the chicken and tomatoes. Garnish with additional asiago cheese.

Buttermilk Dressing

MAKES ABOUT 2 CUPS

$\frac{1}{3}$ cup red onion, minced
2 scallions, thinly sliced
$\frac{1}{2}$ teaspoon Roasted Garlic (page 141), or 1 garlic clove, minced
$\frac{1}{2}$ teaspoon dried thyme, finely chopped
1 cup sour cream
$\frac{3}{4}$ cup buttermilk
$\frac{3}{4}$ cup mayonnaise
1 tablespoon Italian seasoning
1 tablespoon Tabasco sauce
$\frac{1}{4}$ teaspoon garlic powder
$\frac{1}{4}$ teaspoon onion powder
1 tablespoon apple cider vinegar
1 tablespoon red wine vinegar
Kosher salt
Freshly ground black pepper

Whisk together all the ingredients in a bowl. Transfer to an airtight container and refrigerate. Chill for at least 2 hours, and shake vigorously just before serving.

For Chipotle Ranch Dressing, add 1 to 2 puréed chipotle peppers to 1 tablespoon of adobo sauce (the liquid that comes in the can of chipotle peppers) and prepare the same. For Bleu Cheese Buttermilk Dressing, add $\frac{1}{3}$ cup bleu cheese crumbles and prepare the same.

SOUTHWEST SALAD

⟶ SERVES 1 ⟵

We love our Buttermilk Dressing so much, we use it for more than one salad. The typically southwestern flavors in this salad work well with the Ranch-Style Beans, especially if you make the recipe with black beans instead of pinto beans.

2 cups romaine lettuce, chopped
½ cup Ranch-Style Beans (page 67)
½ cup fresh corn
½ cup asiago cheese, grated
1 large chicken breast, grilled or breaded, and sliced in strips
6 to 8 tortilla chips, broken
¼ cup Buttermilk Dressing (page 48)

Toss the romaine with the beans, corn, and cheese in large bowl and mix well. Place on a plate and top with the chicken strips and tortilla chips. Drizzle with the Buttermilk Dressing.

TEXAS WEDGE

→ SERVES 6 ONLY BECAUSE ONCE YOU CUT UP THAT ICEBERG WEDGE,
WE KNOW YOU'LL WANT TO INVITE SOME FRIENDS TO JOIN YOU! →

We think iceberg gets a bad rap. After all, you can't cut those sissy field greens into a big old wedge suitable for a Texas appetite. Here's a way to add a special kick to iceberg with a twist of Pico de Gallo, which always manages to spice things up! Consider topping grilled fish or chicken with our Pico de Gallo or chowing down on this as a dip with your favorite tortilla chips.

1   head iceberg lettuce, cored, and cut into
    6 wedges
1   to 2 cups Pico Vinaigrette
1   cup bleu cheese crumbles

Top each lettuce wedge with a generous ¼ cup of Pico Vinaigrette. Garnish with 1 to 2 tablespoons of bleu cheese crumbles.

Pico Vinaigrette

MAKES 4 CUPS

¼   cup tomato juice
¼   cup apple cider vinegar
2   tablespoons honey
1   egg yolk
2   cups extra virgin olive oil
    Cold water
2   teaspoons kosher salt
¼   teaspoon freshly ground black pepper
1   cup Pico de Gallo

In a large mixing bowl, whisk together the tomato juice, apple cider vinegar, honey, and egg yolk. Pour the mixture into a blender or food processor and slowly add the oil in a thin stream, until the dressing emulsifies and thickens. If the dressing becomes too thick, thin it with water, 1 tablespoon at a time.

Fold in Pico de Gallo, and season the mixture with salt and pepper. Serve immediately, or refrigerate in an airtight container and shake well just before serving.

Pico de Gallo

MAKES 1 CUP

We find that people are kinda crazy about citrus, so be sure that it's got enough lime juice and cilantro for your tastebuds before you add it to the dressing.

1   teaspoon kosher salt
2   roma tomatos, diced
½   red onion, diced
¼   bunch cilantro, roughly chopped
3   jalapeño peppers, seeded and diced
    Juice of 5 limes

Combine all the ingredients in a large bowl and toss well. Serve immediately, or refrigerate in an airtight container and shake well just before serving.

SIDES

BARBARA'S BRAISED CABBAGE

— SERVES 12 —

Barbara is Fred's mom. You remember Fred—he's the one who makes such great gumbo. This braised cabbage is such a treasured Hamilton family secret that we literally had to get on our knees and beg to include it in this cookbook. We know that cabbage doesn't necessarily top most folks' lists of favorite sides, but you've got to try this recipe. There's something about how the cabbage caramelizes with a rich sweet-and-sour flavor that has our customers asking for more every time it's on the menu.

6   bacon slices, raw and diced
1   yellow onion, diced
1   head green cabbage, shredded
1   head red cabbage, shredded
2   cups white wine vinegar
¼   cup Rich Chicken Broth (page 30)
1   cup sugar

In a large stockpot over medium-high heat, sauté the diced bacon until crisp. Add the diced onions and cook until soft and translucent. Add the shredded cabbage, vinegar, and broth, and sauté over high heat for 5 minutes. Add the sugar and continue to cook over high heat, stirring constantly so the sugar doesn't burn. Cook until the sugar becomes caramelized, usually about 5 minutes.

BEST DAMN MACARONI AND CHEESE EVER

Try this mac n'cheese with Pickled Jalapeños—yes, really! Simply make the Reata Pickles but substitute fresh jalapeños for the cucumbers. Pickled or not, the addition of jalapeños and bacon takes this dish way beyond the boxed version we all grew up on. We like to serve this crowd pleaser in small, cast-iron skillets as a side to just about anything during the winter months.

2 cups heavy cream
1/2 cup asiago cheese, grated
1/2 cup Monterey Jack cheese, shredded
4 cups elbow macaroni, cooked and drained
1/4 cup fresh jalapeño peppers, seeded and diced
4 slices bacon, cooked crisp and crumbled
  Kosher salt
  Freshly ground black pepper
2 cups sharp cheddar cheese, shredded
1 1/2 cup dried bread crumbs (optional)

Preheat the oven on the broil setting. Heat a large pot to medium and add the heavy cream. When the cream begins to bubble around the edges, add the grated asiago and shredded Monterey Jack cheeses, stirring constantly until they are completely melted. Fold the cooked macaroni into the creamy cheese mixture and combine until thoroughly incorporated. Add the diced jalapeños and crispy bacon crumbles.

At this point, the cheese mixture should be nicely blended and melted to the point of being stringy. In fact, when you pull out your mixing spoon, the cheese should have the consistency of glue. If the mixture appears too wet, add a little more asiago and Monterey Jack, small handfuls at a time. If the mixture seems too dry, add more heavy cream, 2 tablespoons at a time. Season with salt and pepper. Pour the mixture into a large baking dish and distribute evenly. Top with shredded cheddar (and bread crumbs, if desired).

Place the baking dish under the broiler. Watch it closely. The casserole is done when the shredded cheese on top begins to bubble and the top layer of macaroni starts to brown around the edges. Some folks want their mac n'cheese to rest about 10 minutes before serving, but others like it piping hot right out of the oven.

CORN PUDDING

This dish is so simple—all you do is combine everything into a casserole dish, mix, and bake. It has become a Thanksgiving staple with Julie's family, not only because it's delicious but also because it means fewer dishes to clean up after the football game comes on and the turkey coma kicks in.

2 cups Basic Creamed Corn
1 cup whole milk
3 tablespoons unsalted butter
2 tablespoons cornstarch
2 eggs, beaten well
3/4 cup sugar
2 teaspoons vanilla extract
1/4 dried bread crumbs

Preheat oven to 375 degrees F. In a baking dish, combine all ingredients. Bake for about 30 minutes, then reduce the temperature to 325 degrees F. Bake for 1 hour at the lower temperature. The pudding is done when the casserole is firm in the center. Let the pudding rest for about 10 minutes before serving, so it can solidify just a little bit. Top with a light dusting of dried bread crumbs, and serve.

Basic Creamed Corn

3 tablespoons unsalted butter
3 tablespoons all-purpose flour
1 1/2 cups heavy cream
5 ears fresh corn, shucked, cleaned, and kernels removed
Kosher salt
Freshly ground white pepper

Melt the butter in a heavy skillet over medium heat. Whisk in the flour, blending thoroughly to make a roux, cooking until the flour turns light brown. In a slow, steady stream, pour in the heavy cream, whisking constantly to prevent lumps or scorching. Continue whisking vigorously until all the ingredients are thoroughly combined and the sauce begins to bubble and thicken. Add the corn and simmer over low heat for about 30 minutes, stirring constantly. Remove from the heat and season with salt and pepper.

GRANMA MACKAY'S POTATOES AU GRATIN

◆→ SERVES 10 ◆→

Granma Mackay is my mother's mom, and boy she could make a mean dish of potatoes. My mom and her sister make this casserole a ton, and every time those gals make it, they wonder why their's is just a smidge off their mom's version. Honestly, we could care less—we're just happy to test and retest. Feel free to use mild cheddar if you prefer less sharpness and a creamier taste.

5   fresh russet potatoes, washed, peeled, and cut
      in thirds
      Water
4   cups sharp cheddar cheese, shredded
2½ cups White Sauce
1   teaspoon ground paprika

Preheat the oven to 350 degrees F. In a large stockpot, partially boil the precut potatoes, usually about 10 minutes. The potatoes will continue to bake in the casserole. Drain, and set aside to cool. Butter a large baking dish and set aside. Slice the cooled potatoes into ¼-inch pieces. Place approximately half the potatoes evenly on the bottom of a large baking dish, covering thoroughly. Pour half the reserved White Sauce over the first layer of potatoes. Spread 2 cups of the shredded cheddar over the cream.

Layer the remaining potatoes on top of the shredded cheese and cream. Pour the remaining White Sauce evenly over the dish, completely covering the ingredients. Top with the remaining 2 cups of shredded cheese. Lightly sprinkle with ground paprika. Bake, uncovered, on a baking sheet (to catch the drips), for about 30 to 40 minutes. The potatoes are done when the cheese topping is melted and begins to bubble, and the casserole has slightly browned around the edges.

White Sauce

MAKES ABOUT 2½ CUPS

4   tablespoons unsalted butter
4   tablespoons all-purpose flour
2   cups heavy cream
2   teaspoons Reata Grill Spice (page 138)
      Kosher salt
      Freshly ground black pepper

In a large saucepan, over medium heat, melt the butter. Whisk in the flour, blending thoroughly to make a roux, cooking until the flour turns light brown. Add the cream and Reata Grill Spice and bring the mixture to a boil, stirring constantly to prevent scalding. When the cream reaches the boiling point, stir for 1 minute more. Season with salt and pepper. Remove from the heat and set aside.

PERFECT MASHED POTATOES

— SERVES 6 —

We change the flavor of our mashed potatoes, sometimes garlic, sometimes cheese, every day at the restaurants. Skins on, skins off—that's a personal preference. We mostly do them with the skins off, but lots of our patrons prefer the skins on. Why not try a tater taste-off between a batch with skins and a batch without? For a spectacular party presentation, serve them in martini glasses and let your guests create their own mashed-potato sundae with added toppings, including shredded cheese, crumbled bacon, sour cream, chives, and one of our flavored butters.

5 Idaho potatoes (skins optional)
  Water

Cut the potatoes in half, then cut each half into quarters. In a large stockpot, bring the water to a boil, add the potatoes, and continue boiling over high heat for about 20 to 25 minutes, until the potatoes are fork tender. Drain.

Cream Sauce

8 tablespoons unsalted butter
1 cup heavy cream
  Kosher salt
  Freshly ground black pepper

While the potatoes are boiling, melt the butter in a small saucepan over medium heat. Lower the heat, slowly add the heavy cream, and bring to a simmer, stirring constantly. (If you are going to make a flavored potato, this is when you would add the extra seasoning, spice, or sauce.) Season with salt and pepper. Continue simmering the cream until it has reduced by about 25 percent, and remove from the heat.

Mash the boiled potatoes in the stockpot they were cooked in. While the potatoes are still warm (this is important for the flavor of the cream to be absorbed), add the hot Cream Sauce. Thoroughly combine the Cream Sauce with the potatoes to finish mashing. Serve immediately.

Flavor Variations

Add one, two, or as many combinations you can dream up!

½ bunch fresh cilantro, finely chopped
1 whole head (yes, the whole head!) Roasted Garlic (page 141)
2 to 3 Roasted Shallots (page 132)
3 jalapeño peppers, seeded and minced
¼ cup fresh horseradish, finely grated
2 tablespoons Ancho Chili Cream (page 78)
2 cups grated asiago cheese
2 to 3 cups shredded sharp cheddar cheese
1 cup fresh goat cheese

RANCH-STYLE BEANS

⟶ SERVES 6 ⟶

The original "official" Texas ranch-style beans recipe was first unveiled in 1872 and manufactured right in Fort Worth within smelling distance from the present-day downtown Fort Worth Reata. To this day, we've never gotten our hands on that secret recipe. And even though that local factory has up and gone, we've managed to create a close facsimile. Lately, we've grown quite fond of black beans, so we made this recipe adaptable for either pinto or black beans. And sometimes we even throw in some dark beer when the water starts to boil down as it lends a great flavor.

4 to 5 cups (32-ounce bag) raw pinto beans, or
    black beans
    Water
    Dark beer (optional)
2 tablespoons kosher salt
2 yellow onions, diced
1 whole head garlic, all cloves peeled
    (use procedure for Roasted Garlic, page 141)
½ bunch fresh cilantro, roughly chopped

In a large stockpot, soak the beans in cold water for 24 hours. With the water still covering the beans (they will have absorbed more than you think overnight), add all the remaining ingredients to the pot. Cook the beans over low heat for 2 to 3 hours, adding water (or beer), as needed, so beans remain submerged while the mixture simmers. The beans are done when they are soft and tender, but still hold their individual shape. Add the chopped cilantro, stir well, and serve.

TENDERLOIN-WRAPPED ASPARAGUS

◆—► SERVES 6 ◄—◆

Not only is this a great side that's pretty to look at, it also makes great party food. You do have to freeze the tenderloin a few hours first, so make it as a second appetizer when you are already preparing the Tenderloin Carpaccio because that recipe uses frozen beef as well.

12   stems fresh asparagus, ends trimmed
      Water
 6   ounces (about 1 small filet) beef tenderloin,
      well trimmed
¼   to ½ cup Sweet Molasses Glaze (page 19),
      for drizzling

Place the tenderloin in the freezer for at least 4 hours. Bring a large stockpot of water to a rapid boil. Add the trimmed asparagus and boil for about 2 minutes. Quickly remove the asparagus and toss in a large bowl filled with ice-cold water.

Remove the tenderloin from the freezer. For easy slicing, the tenderloin should be fairly hard, but not frozen solid. Use a mandolin, or a steady hand and an extremely sharp knife, to slice the still-frozen tenderloin into 12 very thin strips about ⅛ to ¼ inch thick. Unlike the Tenderloin Carpaccio, the meat does not have to be paper thin.

Place the slices of tenderloin on a platter to thaw (this should only take a few minutes). When the beef strips are thawed, wrap each strip around a blanched asparagus spear. Grill the wrapped asparagus on a preheated medium grill for about 5 minutes, rotating frequently, until most of the pink color is gone from the beef and the asparagus begins to char just slightly. Drizzle with Sweet Molasses Glaze immediately before serving.

MAINS

BARBECUE SHRIMP ENCHILADAS - 72
Sautéed Shrimp
Barbecue Enchilada Sauce

**FISH TACOS WITH CHIPOTLE CREAM AND
ROASTED CORN RELISH - 74**
Chipotle Cream
Roasted Corn Relish

**BLACKENED BUFFALO RIB EYE WITH
RASPBERRY-CHIPOTLE BUTTER - 77**
Raspberry-Chipotle Butter

**CARNE ASADA WITH CHEESE ENCHILADAS AND
ANCHO CHILI CREAM - 78**
Cheese Enchiladas
Ancho Chili Cream
Skirt Steak in Cerveza Soak

**CF CHICKEN-FRIED STEAK WITH
CRACKED-PEPPER CREAM GRAVY - 83**
Cracked-Pepper Cream Gravy

CHICKEN CHILI RELLENOS - 84
Shredded Chicken from the Grill
Roasted Poblano Peppers

GARLIC-CRUSTED PRIME RIB - 87
Prime Rib with Dry Rub

JANE'S CHIPOTLE MEATLOAF - 88
Mushroom Gravy

JUSTIN TIME CHICKEN POT PIE - 90

**MAPLE DUCK BREAST WITH
SAGE BROWN BUTTER SAUCE - 93**
Sage Brown Butter Sauce

**PAN-SEARED PEPPER-CRUSTED TENDERLOIN
WITH PORT WINE GLAZE - 94**
Port Wine Glaze

**RODEO RIB EYE WITH
JALAPEÑO-CILANTRO BUTTER - 99**
Jalapeño-Cilantro Butter

**PECAN-CRUSTED CHICKEN WITH
RASPBERRY-CHIPOTLE CREAM - 100**
Crushed Pecan Coating
Raspberry-Chipotle Cream

PORK CHOPS WITH SPICED-PEAR RUM SAUCE - 103
Citrus Soak
Spiced-Pear Rum Sauce

STACKED CHICKEN ENCHILADAS - 104
Tomatillo Sauce

PISTACHIO-CRUSTED TILAPIA - 106

**VENISON CHOPS WITH BERRY GOOD
GAME SAUCE - 107**
Berry Good Game Sauce

BARBECUE SHRIMP ENCHILADAS

→► SERVES 6 ◄←

From time to time we like to mix it up a little. This recipe has been on our menu forever, so one day somebody had the bright idea to change a few things around and remove it for a season or two. What a mistake! You could hear the cowgirls howling from Fort Worth to Big Bend. Suffice it say, we've learned our lesson.

12 (8-inch) flour tortillas
4 cups Barbecue Enchilada Sauce
3 to 4 cups Monterey Jack cheese, shredded
1½ pounds Sautéed Shrimp

Preheat the oven to 350 degrees F. Lightly coat the bottom of a large baking dish with about ½ cup of the Barbecue Enchilada Sauce

Enchilada Assembly

Cut a ½-inch strip from the side of each flour tortilla and discard. Pour about 1 tablespoon of Barbecue Enchilada Sauce in a straight line, through the center of each tortilla. Place about 4 or 5 of the cooked shrimp on top of the sauce. Sprinkle 2 heaping tablespoons of the shredded cheese on the cooked shrimp. Roll the tortilla tightly (like a small burrito) and place in a baking dish that has been coated with Barbecue Enchilada Sauce.

Nestle the 12 assembled enchiladas side-by-side in the coated baking dish. Pour the remaining 1½ cups of Barbecue Enchilada Sauce over the enchiladas. Sprinkle the remaining ¾ to 1 cup shredded cheese over the sauce. Cover loosely with aluminum foil, so the cheese doesn't stick to the foil.

Bake in the preheated oven for about 15 minutes, or until the cheese topping begins to bubble and the edges of the enchiladas turn a little crusty. Remove from the oven and let rest about 5 to 10 minutes before serving.

Sautéed Shrimp

¼ cup oil, for sautéing
2 tablespoons fresh garlic, minced
1½ pounds (sized 41 to 50 per pound) fresh shrimp, raw, peeled, deveined, and deheaded
    Kosher salt
    Freshly ground black pepper

Coat a large sauté pan with oil and heat over medium-high heat. Add the garlic and sauté until the garlic is toasted to a rich brown color. Add the shrimp to the sauté pan. Immediately dust the entire pan with salt and pepper to lightly coat the shrimp. Sauté the shrimp for about 3 to 4 minutes, stirring often. (The goal is for the shrimp to be cooked to a medium temperature when assembled in the enchiladas. Baking the enchiladas will cook the shrimp a little more.)

continued

Barbecue Enchilada Sauce

MAKES 4 CUPS

 3 cups ketchup
 4 tablespoons apple cider vinegar
 1/2 cup brown sugar
 2 teaspoons Tabasco sauce
 1 tablespoon Worcestershire sauce
 3/4 cup yellow onion, diced
 1 dried bay leaf

 1/2 teaspoon ground espresso beans
 1 cup heavy cream

Place all the ingredients in a saucepan over medium-high heat and bring to a rapid boil. Reduce the heat to low and simmer for 10 minutes. Remove the pan from the heat and let the mixture cool thoroughly. Allowing it to thicken will make assembling the enchiladas easier.

FISH TACOS WITH CHIPOTLE CREAM AND ROASTED CORN RELISH

← SERVES 6, 3 TACOS PER SERVING →

My dad and I love to fish and try to get out on the water at least 30 days out of the year. We tell everyone a lot of business gets done out on the boat, but who are we kidding? We recommend using tilapia, cod, or red snapper for these tacos. You can also make a healthier variation by grilling your fish instead of frying.

Frying the Fish

 Egg Wash (page 140)
 4 cups Reata Flour Spice (page 138)
 2 pounds fresh white fish, cut into about 1/2-inch-wide strips
 1 1/2 cups peanut oil, for frying

Dredge each piece of fish in the Egg Wash, then toss in the Reata Flour Spice, generously coating each. In a cast-iron, deep-sided skillet, heat the oil to about 350 degrees F. Pan-fry the fish strips until they're golden brown on each side, turning only once, usually about 3 to 4 minutes per side, depending on your frying apparatus and the thickness of the filets. Drain the cooked fish on paper towels. Reserve the fish in a baking dish in a warm oven, and reserve the skillet with the frying oil, until you're ready to assemble the tacos.

Assembling the Tacos

 18 corn tortillas
 2 pounds fresh white fish, cooked, and cut into 2-inch strips
 3 cups Zesty Corn Relish
 3 to 4 cups iceberg lettuce, shredded
 1 1/2 cups Chipotle Cream
 2 limes, cut into wedges

Reheat the frying oil over medium-low heat. Place the corn tortillas in the skillet, one at a time, turning once, about 5 seconds per side, just enough to make them pliable. Place the warm tortillas on a baking sheet covered with paper towels to drain.

Place a fish strip in the center of each tortilla. Top the fish with about 1 tablespoon of Roasted

Corn Relish. Fill each tortilla with shredded lettuce. Drizzle with Chipotle Cream, and serve with a wedge of fresh lime.

Chipotle Cream

MAKES ABOUT 1 CUP

You can make this as hot as you like based on the number of chipotle peppers you use. Some folks are brave enough to use a whole can, but these are the folks who like to show off (and sweat)! We think this spicy cream is mighty fine when tossed with pasta or drizzled on top of Carne Asada as an alternate to the Crème Fraiche.

3   chipotle peppers, with the adobo sauce
1/4   cup brown sugar
3/4   cups heavy cream
1   teaspoon kosher salt

In a small saucepan, combine the chipotle peppers in adobo sauce with the brown sugar over medium-low heat. When the brown sugar has thoroughly melted, stir well, and slowly add the heavy cream and the salt. Remove from the heat and transfer the mixture to a blender or food processor, setting aside the saucepan. Purée the mixture, and return it to the saucepan. Simmer over low heat until the sauce reduces by about 25 percent.

Roasted Corn Relish

MAKES ABOUT 3 CUPS

We've said it before and we'll say it again: roasting is so easy. When the oven or grill heats up your produce, the natural sugars caramelize and enrich the natural flavors enough that they run smack dab into your tasters. You'll find instructions for roasting fresh poblano peppers (red bell peppers are prepared the same way) with the Chicken Chile Rellenos. By the by, one good-sized ear of fresh corn yields about 1/2 cup roasted corn. This is also a tasty dipping salsa for Tortilla Crisps.

6   ears fresh corn, off the cob, or 2 (15-ounce) cans, drained
3/4   cup extra virgin olive oil
    Kosher salt
    Freshly ground black pepper
2   roma tomatoes, diced
1   bunch cilantro, roughly chopped
2   jalapeño peppers, seeded and minced

Preheat the oven to a broil setting. In a large bowl, combine the corn, 1/4 cup of the olive oil, the salt, and pepper. Thinly spread the corn mixture on a baking sheet and roast under the broiler for about 5 to 10 minutes, stirring often. The corn has roasted evenly when the kernels turn a uniform rich brown color. Remove the corn from the oven, drain, discard the extra oil, and let cool on the baking sheet.

In a large bowl, combine the remaining ingredients (including the remaining 1/2 cup of olive oil). Add the roasted corn to the tomato mixture and toss to combine. Season with salt and pepper. Chill for at least 3 to 4 hours before serving.

BLACKENED BUFFALO RIB EYE WITH RASPBERRY-CHIPOTLE BUTTER

Not only is the taste of buffalo fantastic, the meat is much lower in fat and cholesterol than either beef or chicken, and it contains more protein and fewer calories. Perfect Mashed Potatoes make a swell sidekick to this steak. We're partial to the Roasted Garlic variation, because a mound of them is just right when paired with the sweet spiciness of the Raspberry-Chipotle Butter atop the rib eye. Because buffalo is so lean, we recommend cooking to a medium-rare temperature so the meat stays juicy and flavorful.

2 tablespoons oil, for sautéing
1/2 cup Reata Blackening Seasoning (page 136)
6 (10-ounce) buffalo rib eye steaks
Kosher salt
Freshly ground black pepper
3/4 cup Raspberry-Chipotle Butter (As the mixture reheats, it will spread and flatten even more.)

Preheat the oven to 300 degrees F. Dredge each steak in the Reata Blackening Seasoning, coating generously on each side. Heat a large sauté pan over high heat and add the oil when hot. Place each steak in the hot pan and briefly sear on high, just until the meat begins to caramelize, only about 1 to 2 minutes. Turn, and sauté 1 to 2 minutes on the other side.

Finish the steaks in a baking dish in the preheated oven until all the steaks are cooked to your preferred temperature. Season with salt and pepper. Serve each steak warm, topped with 2 tablespoons of Raspberry-Chipotle Butter.

Raspberry-Chipotle Butter

MAKES ABOUT 1 CUP

It's a good idea to make flavored butters in large batches and freeze for later use. Simply chill the blended butter in the refrigerator for about 30 minutes, and then roll it into a medium-sized log on wax paper. Tightly wrap the log in the wax paper, twist the ends closed, and freeze. When you're ready to use the butter, remove from the freezer and slice off rounds as needed. Don't be afraid to experiment with your own flavor combinations—the possibilities literally are limitless!

1 pound unsalted butter, softened to room temperature
1 chipotle pepper, seeded and minced
1 shallot, peeled and minced
1/4 cup fresh raspberries, puréed
1 tablespoon kosher salt
1 tablespoon freshly ground black pepper

Place all the ingredients in a food processor, and blend until thoroughly incorporated.

CARNE ASADA WITH CHEESE ENCHILADAS AND ANCHO CHILI CREAM

← SERVES 6 →

When we think about Juan Jaramillo, we think about Carne Asada. Juan actually sent this out as the last dish we served right before the tornado came calling in March of 2000. Chef Juan has been with our Fort Worth restaurant for more than a decade, and he's literally the whole enchilada. He's simply the best guy in town for pairing the most unlikely people in the kitchen for top-notch menu items. Juan makes matches in the kitchen that are truly unbeatable. Serve this recipe with Ranch-Style Beans, add your favorite Spanish rice, and watch your family run like the wind to the table.

Cheese Enchiladas

- 12 corn tortillas
- 4 cups Ancho Chili Cream
- 3 to 4 cups Monterey Jack cheese, shredded

Preheat the oven to 350 degrees F. Lightly coat the bottom of a large baking dish with about ½ cup of the Ancho Chili Cream.

Enchilada Assembly

Pour about 1 tablespoon of Ancho Chili Cream in a straight line down the center of each tortilla. Sprinkle 2 heaping tablespoons of the shredded cheese over the cream sauce. Roll up the tortilla tightly (like a small burrito) and place in a shallow baking dish that has been coated with Ancho Chili Cream.

Nestle the 12 assembled enchiladas side-by-side in the coated baking dish. Pour the remaining 1½ cups Ancho Chili Cream over the enchiladas. Sprinkle the remaining ¾ to 1 cup of the shredded cheese over the sauce. Cover loosely with aluminum foil, so the cheese doesn't stick to the foil.

Bake in the preheated oven for about 15 minutes, or until the cheese on top begins to bubble and the edges of the enchiladas turn a little crusty. Remove from the oven and let rest about 5 to 10 minutes before serving.

Ancho Chili Cream

MAKES 4 CUPS

The bitterness of ancho chili peppers varies, but you can easily adjust the taste with an additional teaspoon or two of honey. When you leave out the heavy cream, this mixture becomes the Ancho Chili Sauce that is used in the Chicken Chili Rellenos.

- 16 dried ancho chili peppers, seeded
- 6 to 8 garlic cloves, minced
- ½ yellow onion, diced
- ⅓ cup honey
- 2 cups water
- 1½ tablespoons ground cumin
- 1 roma tomato, diced
- 1 cup heavy cream

Rinse the chili peppers under cold running water, making sure all the seeds are removed.

continued

Place the peppers, garlic, onions, cumin, and honey in a large stockpot. Add the water and cook over medium-high heat for 30 minutes. Remove the pot from the heat and add the diced tomato. Let the mixture cool thoroughly. When thoroughly cooled, place in a food processor or blender, and purée until fairly smooth.

Strain the liquid through a fine mesh strainer to remove any remaining pulp or seeds. Place the strained liquid in a saucepan, add the heavy cream, and bring it to a rolling boil. Reduce the heat to low and simmer for 10 minutes. Remove the pan from the heat and let the mixture cool thoroughly. Allowing it to thicken will make assembling the enchiladas easier.

Skirt Steak in Cerveza Soak

To make a steak that will really blow your skirt up, it's important to trim off all the white sinuous membrane before marinating.

    4   pounds skirt steak
    1   bottle Corona beer
        Juice of 2 limes
    1/2 cup canola oil

Marinate the steaks in the beer, lime juice, and oil for at least 4 hours, but preferably overnight for moist, tender beef. Remove from the marinade and grill over high heat, about 5 to 6 minutes on each side, for medium-rare steaks. This cut of meat can get a bit tough if it's overcooked, so avoid leaving it too long on the grill.

Building the Carne Asada

THE FOLLOWING INGREDIENTS ARE PER SERVING

    2   Cheese Enchiladas
    8   to 12 ounces beef fajita steak
    1/4 cup Great Guacamole (page 2)
    1/4 cup Pico de Gallo (page 55)

Place the cooked fajita steak on each plate. Top each steak with 2 warm Cheese Enchiladas. Garnish with a generous 1/4-cup dollop of Great Guacamole with 1/4 cup Pico de Gallo on the side.

Thumb to index finger = rare

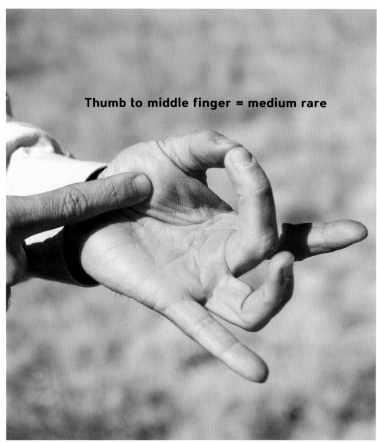

Thumb to middle finger = medium rare

A simple method we use at Reata to tell when a steak or other type of meat is cooked to the desired temperature without cutting into it is to press on it with tongs and feel how much the meat compresses with a given amount of pressure. This correlates to pressing your finger onto the meaty part of your palm when your thumb and other fingers are touching.

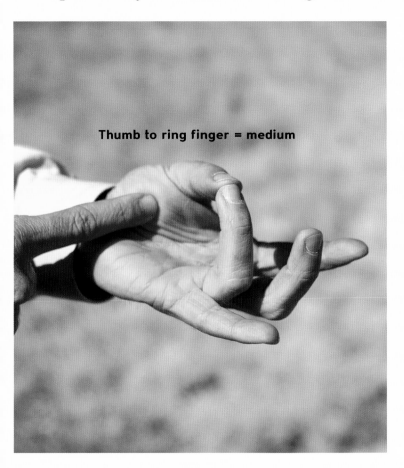

Thumb to ring finger = medium

Thumb to pinkie finger = well done

CF CHICKEN-FRIED STEAK WITH CRACKED-PEPPER CREAM GRAVY

My father loves his homestead, the CF Ranch. Located in the Davis Mountains of West Texas, the topography was created 35 million years ago when the Paisano Volcano erupted with a force 1,000 times greater than that of Mount St. Helens to create the most beautiful mountains and valleys you've seen this side of the border. He'll deny it all day long that CF stands for "Chicken-Fried." But when you've got a piece of crusty, batter-dipped beef that's so big it falls off the side of a jumbo dinner plate, why wouldn't you call attention to it? Pair it with a mountain of Perfect Mashed Potatoes and a valley of Cracked-Pepper Cream Gravy, and you're all set for a siesta at your very own homestead.

6   (8-ounce) beef cutlets, tenderized
    Egg Wash (page 140)
3   cups Reata Flour Spice (page 138)
    Peanut oil, for frying
3   cups Cracked-Pepper Cream Gravy

Dredge each cutlet in Egg Wash, then toss in Reata Flour Spice, generously coating each piece. In a cast-iron skillet or deep fryer, heat the oil to about 350 degrees F. Cook the cutlets until they are golden brown all over, turning them once, usually about 5 minutes per side, depending on your frying apparatus and the thickness of the cutlets.

Drain the cutlets on paper towels. Serve immediately, or reserve them in a baking dish in a warm oven. Serve with about ½ cup of the Cracked-Pepper Cream Gravy ladled over each steak.

Cracked-Pepper Cream Gravy

MAKES ABOUT 4 CUPS

Our cream gravy is pure rich, thick, gooey goodness for topping anything that's fried and crunchy. We know some folks who even dip their potatoes in it. If for some crazy reason the gravy appears a little too thin, just whip up more roux with a touch more butter and flour to make your goodness perfect.

2   sticks unsalted butter
1   cup all-purpose flour
1   quart whole milk
2   teaspoons kosher salt
2   teaspoons freshly ground black pepper

In a large, heavy skillet, melt the butter over medium heat. Whisk in the flour, a little at a time, to make a roux, whisking constantly. Cook for 5 minutes, whisking often, until the flour turns golden brown. Slowly add the milk, while continuing to whisk to avoid lumps or a pasty texture. Add the salt and pepper. Continue cooking over medium-low heat for 15 minutes, stirring often to keep the gravy from scorching or sticking to the pan.

CHICKEN CHILI RELLENOS

→ SERVES 6 →

With a large enough pan, you can use three whole chickens (leave the skin on) in place of purchasing the legs and thighs separately. If you're short on time, go ahead and use two store-bought rotisserie chickens in place of the Shredded Chicken. Drizzling the top of each relleno with some of our Crème Fraiche and a scoop of Great Guacamole will mellow the pepper just enough to keep from setting your mouth on fire. Believe it or not, some folks even batter and fry these. If decadence is your thing, just dredge in some Egg Wash and Reata Flour Spice a few times to make a generous crust before you fry. Regardless, we say serve with your favorite Spanish rice and some Ranch-Style Beans.

Shredded Chicken from the Grill

1/4 cup oil, for braising
12 chicken legs and thighs, with skin on
Water
1/2 cup kosher salt
1 tablespoon ground cumin

Place the oil in a braising pan and heat over a piping-hot grill. When the oil begins to sizzle, add the chicken. Cover with water, making sure the chicken remains submerged throughout the cooking process. Generously sprinkle with salt and cumin. Lower the heat to medium-high, so the water continues to simmer. Move the braising pan to the grill and continue cooking for about 30 to 45 minutes over a medium grill, replenishing the water in the pan as needed.

The chicken is done when it is firm and white on the outside, and when you slice into it, there is no pink to be seen. Remove the braising pan from grill and carefully drain the broth and discard. Let the chicken cool thoroughly. Remove the chicken skin and bones, and discard before shredding the meat. Shred the chicken, and reserve.

Roasted Poblano Peppers

12 poblano peppers
1/4 cup canola oil

Rub the oil liberally over the poblano peppers. Roast the peppers directly on grill grate until they are charred, turning frequently to ensure charring on all sides. Place the warm roasted peppers in a large bowl and tightly cover with plastic wrap for about 15 minutes, until they begin to "sweat."

Peel off the first layer of skin from each pepper. Slit the peppers lengthwise, rinse under cold water to remove the seeds, and reserve.

Stuffing the Rellenos

4 cups goat cheese
4 cups Monterey Jack cheese, shredded
6 roma tomatoes, diced
3 pounds reserved Shredded Chicken from the Grill
2 cups Ancho Chili Sauce (page 78—prepare the Ancho Chili Cream but omit the heavy cream)
12 Roasted Poblano Peppers

continued

Preheat the oven to 350 degrees F. In a large bowl, combine the cheeses and thoroughly mix. In another large bowl, add the diced tomatoes and shredded chicken, and thoroughly combine. Add the Ancho Chili Sauce to the chicken and tomatoes and mix until all the ingredients are well combined. Carefully fill each pepper with about 1 cup of the chicken-tomato-chili mixture.

Top each stuffed pepper with ½ cup of the blended cheeses. Place each stuffed pepper, cheese-side up, in a large baking dish. Bake in the preheated oven for about 20 minutes, or until the cheese topping is melted and beginning to bubble. Serve 2 rellenos per person, drizzled with 1 to 2 tablespoons of Crème Fraiche and a generous side of Great Guacamole.

GARLIC-CRUSTED PRIME RIB

Good things come to those who wait, so be sure and plan a day ahead of time for this delectable dish. To make mouthwatering meat, it really needs to absorb the flavors from the horseradish and garlic by chilling overnight. If you haven't banked on quite so much prep time, try our Prime Rib with Dry Rub instead. For either recipe, the difference in the number of servings they'll yield depends on the size of the cut of meat you purchase. If you adjust the cut, plan to roast it for about 15 minutes per pound in a 350-degree-F oven.

1 (6-pound) boneless beef rib roast, well trimmed
30 garlic cloves, unpeeled and whole
1/4 cup extra virgin olive oil
1/3 cup fresh horseradish, grated
Kosher salt
Freshly ground black pepper

Preparing the Prime Rib

Preheat the oven to 350 degrees F. Toss the garlic cloves and olive oil in a small baking dish, and tightly cover with aluminum foil. Bake the garlic for about 30 minutes, or until it turns light brown. Remove from the oven, and let cool for about 15 minutes. Peel the outer skin from the garlic, and discard. Combine the olive oil, horseradish, and salt in a food processor. Add the peeled garlic, and purée the mixture until almost smooth.

Place a baking rack on a large, rimmed baking sheet. Generously season the rib roast with salt and pepper on all sides. Coat one side of the roast with a thin layer of the garlic paste and place, paste-side down, on the rack. Paint the top and sides of the roast with the remaining garlic paste. Tightly cover the entire roast and exposed baking sheet with plastic wrap and refrigerate overnight.

Roasting the Prime Rib

Preheat the oven to 350 degrees F. Place the prime rib on the lowest rack possible, and cook until a meat thermometer inserted into the top-center of the roast registers 125 degrees F, usually about 1 hour and 45 minutes, but start checking at about 90 minutes. The center portion of the prime rib will be cooked rare, with the ends being medium to medium-well. Remove the roast from the oven and gently transfer from the rack to a large serving platter. Let it rest for about 30 minutes.

Pour the drippings from the baking sheet into a small saucepan. Reheat the drippings to drizzle over the prime rib just before serving.

Prime Rib with Dry Rub

SERVES 10 TO 12

2 tablespoons Reata Grill Spice (page 138)
2 tablespoons kosher salt, or to taste
2 tablespoons freshly ground black pepper, or to taste
1 (8-pound) boneless beef rib roast, well trimmed
3 tablespoons canola oil

continued

Preheat the oven to a broil setting. If you have two ovens, set one to 350 degrees F. If not, allow the oven to cool briefly after broiling, then reheat to 350 degrees F. Combine the Reata Grill Spice, salt, and pepper in a small bowl. Massage the oil into all sides of the roast, then generously coat the meat with the dry seasoning blend.

Place a baking rack on a large, rimmed baking sheet and place the roast in the center of the rack. Broil the roast for 5 to 10 minutes, until the meat develops a toasty crust. Remove the roast from the broiler, and place on the lowest rack possible (in your second oven or in the reheated oven). Cook at 350 degrees F until a meat thermometer inserted into the top-center of the roast registers 125 degrees F, usually about 1 hour and 45 minutes, but you should start checking at about 90 minutes. The center portion of the prime rib will be cooked rare, with the ends being medium to medium-well.

Remove the roast from the oven, and transfer from the rack to a large serving platter. Let it rest for about 30 minutes. Pour the drippings from the baking sheet into a small saucepan. Reheat the drippings to drizzle over the prime rib just before serving.

JANE'S CHIPOTLE MEATLOAF

SERVES 8

My mother Jane raised us—Amanda, Sarah, and me—on this Micallef house staple. Now that we're all grown and gone, my father has to head to Reata to get his meatloaf fix. At the restaurant, we serve ours right smack dab in the middle of a big old creamy boat of our Perfect Mashed Potatoes.

3	pounds ground beef
2	tablespoons Worcestershire sauce
3	eggs
1	red bell pepper, seeded and diced
1/2	yellow onion, diced
2	green onions, sliced to 1/4 inch
1	tablespoon fresh garlic, minced
2	tablespoons Tabasco sauce
2	tablespoons adobo sauce (from a can of chipotle peppers)
2/3	cup dried bread crumbs
1	tablespoon kosher salt
1	teaspoon freshly ground black pepper

Preheat the oven to 350 degrees F. Place all the ingredients in a large bowl and thoroughly combine.

Fill a large loaf pan (or two small ones—this freezes beautifully, so make an extra for a busy night), and cover the top tightly to seal with aluminum foil. Bake for about 90 minutes, until the top has a light brown crust and the edges are pulling away from the pan. Remove from the meat loaf oven, and let rest for about 10 minutes. Serve with about 1/2 cup Mushroom Gravy.

Mushroom Gravy

MAKES 4 CUPS

4	cups Rich Chicken Broth (page 30)
4	cups Veal Stock (page 145)
1	teaspoon tomato paste
1½	pounds fresh mushrooms, sliced to ¼-inch thickness (we recommend a combination of button, crimini, and baby bella)
¼	yellow onion, diced
½	teaspoon fresh garlic, minced
7	tablespoons unsalted butter
¾	cup all-purpose flour
	Kosher salt
	Freshly ground black pepper

Combine the Rich Chicken Broth, Veal Stock, and tomato paste in a large stockpot over high heat and bring to a boil. Lower the heat to medium and simmer to reduce the liquid by about 50 percent, about 1 hour. In a large sauté pan, combine the mushrooms, onions, and garlic. Add 3 tablespoons of the butter and cook over high heat. When the mushrooms have browned, remove from the heat, and reserve.

In a large saucepan, melt the remaining butter. Whisk in the flour, a little at a time, to make a roux, and cook for about 10 minutes, or until the mixture turns light brown. Remove the roux from the heat and let cool. Return the reserved, reduced stock to a boil. Add the cooled roux to the boiling stock, stirring to avoid lumps. Reduce the heat, and let simmer until the gravy thickens. Add the sautéed mushrooms, and season with salt and pepper.

JUSTIN TIME CHICKEN POT PIE

The good folks from the Justin Boot Company have been friends of Reata since the get-go. Located in Fort Worth since 1925, the company is an institution that upholds the standards and spirit of true Western generosity. Our Fort Worth restaurant has a private room showcasing a few of the most original Justin boots around, including one on a roller skate and another with golf spikes! But the truth is our all-time favorite boots are a pair of soft and supple old ropers. They're timeless classics, just like our Justin Time Chicken Pot Pie.

If you're a little pressed for time, ready-made refrigerated puff-pastry dough will work just fine perched atop this hearty chicken stew. But for those of you who want the honest-to-goodness real pot pie presentation, you know that you have to have both top and bottom crusts. If your family needs two crusts, then Julie's Mom's Pie Crust is perfect for your pie.

3 pounds chicken breasts
2 quarts Rich Chicken Broth (page 30)
4 fresh carrots, diced
4 celery stalks, diced
1 cup fresh corn
1 yellow onion, diced
1 tablespoon fresh garlic, minced
2 tablespoons dried thyme
1/2 bunch cilantro, finely chopped
1 teaspoon kosher salt
1/4 teaspoon freshly ground black pepper
2 sticks unsalted butter
2 cups all-purpose flour
1 Roasted Poblano Pepper (page 84), skinned and diced

In a large stockpot over high heat, boil the chicken breasts in Rich Chicken Broth for about 30 to 45 minutes. The chicken is done when it is firm and white on the outside, and when you slice into it, there is no pink to be seen. Remove from the heat, and gently transfer the cooked chicken to a plate to cool, reserving the chicken stock.

In a large skillet over medium-high heat, sauté the carrots, celery, corn, onion, and garlic for about 10 minutes. Add the thyme, cilantro, 1/2 teaspoon salt, and 1/8 teaspoon pepper. In a separate saucepan over medium heat, melt the butter. Whisk in the flour, a little at a time, to make a roux, cooking for about 10 minutes or until the mixture turns golden brown. Remove from the heat and let cool. Return the chicken stock to a rolling boil.

Add the sautéed vegetables to the boiling stock, then slowly add the roux, a little at a time, to thicken. Thoroughly mix the roux into the stock to ensure the mixture doesn't develop any lumps. Lower the heat, and add the poblano pepper. Dice or shred the cooled chicken, and add to the stock.

Potting the Pie

If you're a two-crust family, make Julie's Mom's Pie Crust according to the recipe. When the bottom crust is lightly baked, fill the shell with the chicken stew, then place the top crust over the dish. Crimp the sides together with a fork, and poke a few holes into the top crust to allow the steam to escape during baking. Bake at 350 degrees F for about 20 minutes, or until the top crust turns golden brown. Let rest, about 10 minutes, before serving.

If you're using a ready-made refrigerated puff pastry, prepare according to the package directions. Ladle about 1 to 1½ cups of the chicken stew into a large bowl and top with the pastry.

MAPLE DUCK BREAST WITH SAGE BROWN BUTTER SAUCE

→ SERVES 6 →

There's simply no comparison between real maple syrup and that awful stuff that dribbles out of a plastic bottle. Duck generally has a strong flavor, so the rich, sweet syrup helps tame the bird just a bit. If you shoot a wild duck, serve two small breasts per person. But if they're store bought, they're usually larger, about 6 to 8 ounces per breast.

6   (6- to 8-ounce) fresh duck breasts, marinated, and with the fat scored
2¹⁄₂   tablespoons unsalted butter

Preheat the oven to 350 degrees F. In a large sauté pan, heat the butter over medium heat. Add 1 duck breast, fat-side down, and sear until crispy and golden brown, turning once, about 3 to 4 minutes per side. Remove the duck breast, and reserve in a baking dish. Repeat until all the breasts are seared on both sides. Remove the sauté pan from the heat, and set aside.

Finish the duck by baking in the preheated oven for about 8 to 10 minutes, or until the duck is firm to the touch and golden brown. Remove from the oven and let rest about 5 minutes. Serve with 2 tablespoons of the Sage Brown Butter Sauce drizzled over each breast.

Maple Marinade

MAKES 3 CUPS

1   cup orange juice, preferably fresh squeezed
1   cup real maple syrup
1   cup Rich Chicken Broth (page 30)

In a large bowl, combine all the liquids. Marinate the duck for at least 2 hours.

Sage Brown Butter Sauce

MAKES 1¹⁄₂ CUPS

¹⁄₂   cup white wine
2   fresh shallots, chopped
3   garlic cloves, minced
2   sticks unsalted butter
2   tablespoons fresh sage, finely chopped (fresh sage is a must here, as dried won't impart the same flavor)

In the reserved sauté pan, reheat the duck drippings over medium heat. Deglaze the pan with the white wine. Add the shallots and garlic, and sauté over medium heat until the sauce becomes fairly clear. Reduce the sauce by about 50 percent over low heat. Add the butter and sage, and cook until the sauce turns golden brown. Pour over the sliced duck breasts.

PAN-SEARED PEPPER-CRUSTED TENDERLOIN WITH PORT WINE GLAZE

→← SERVES 6 →←

Our all-time, number-one, best-selling dish. We predict once you've had your tenderloin glazed with port wine, nothing else will *ever* do. The black pepper for the coating must be coarse and freshly ground, and for goodness sakes, please don't let the amount of pepper scare you away. We promise it makes the meat melt-in-your-mouth good!

6 (8- to 10-ounce) beef tenderloins, well trimmed
12 tablespoons cracked black pepper, or coarsely ground
Kosher salt
2 to 3 tablespoons oil, for sautéing
2 cups Port Wine Glaze

Preheat the oven to 350 degrees F. Generously coat both sides of each tenderloin with the cracked pepper. Season each side with salt. Heat a dry sauté pan to smoking hot. Add the oil 1 to 2 tablespoons at a time. When the oil is hot, add the crusted tenderloin and sear for about 3 minutes. This is really important, because a good, hot sear holds in the juices. Turn the steak and sear 3 minutes more on the other side. Repeat for all 6 steaks.

Reserve the seared steaks in a baking dish. Remove the sauté pan from the heat and set aside to use with the sauce.

Finish the steaks in the preheated oven for 8 to 10 minutes, to achieve medium-rare temperature. Serve immediately on a bed of about ⅓ cup of the Port Wine Glaze.

Port Wine Glaze

MAKES ABOUT 2 CUPS

½ (750-milliliter) bottle port wine (Because the sauce reduces so much, an inexpensive bottle is fine.)
⅓ cup honey
2 quarts Veal Stock (page 145)

Combine all the ingredients in a large stockpot. Cook over high heat for about 1 hour, until the liquid has reduced by about 75 percent and is the consistency of syrup.

RODEO RIB EYE WITH JALAPEÑO-CILANTRO BUTTER

→ SERVES 6 →

Cowtown held its first Fat Stock Show in 1896. Today, the Fort Worth Stock Show & Rodeo is an annual Texas tradition beginning the second weekend in January. Reata jumped aboard the rodeo wagon in 2002 when we opened Reata at the Rodeo, a full-service restaurant and bar on the grounds of the show. The cowboys were so happy, we expanded with a second restaurant and bar, Reata at the Backstage, that overlooks the coliseum. Whether we're at the rodeo or one of our permanent restaurants, Reata always cuts your rib eye to order by hand, including a 64-ouncer that was requested not too long ago!

6   (14- to 18-ounce) beef rib eyes, well trimmed
2   tablespoons Reata Grill Spice (page 138)
1   yellow onion
6   tablespoons unsalted butter, melted for basting
¾   cup Jalapeño–Cilantro Butter

Lightly dust both sides of each rib eye with the Reata Grill Spice. Heat the grill to high. Slice the onion in half and imbed a fork into the rounded end. Run the flat side of the onion over the hot grate to lightly season the grill. Place the steaks on the grill. To make distinct grill marks, rotate each steak at a 90-degree angle after about 2 minutes. After another 2 to 3 minutes, turn over to grill the other side, basting often with the melted butter to ensure the meat stays moist. Cooking time is for medium-rare steak — exactly how we like steak! Serve topped with about 2 tablespoons of Jalapeño-Cilantro Butter.

Jalapeño-Cilantro Butter

MAKES ABOUT 1 CUP

Like the Raspberry-Chipotle Butter we use on the Blackened Buffalo Rib Eye, it's a good idea to make a large batch and freeze for future use. We think flavored butters are great toppers for steaks, but you can also use them on Buttermilk Pecan Biscuits. Simply chill the blended butter in the refrigerator for about 30 minutes, then roll it into a medium-sized log on wax paper. Tightly wrap the log in the wax paper, twist the ends, and freeze. When you're ready to use it, remove from freezer and slice off rounds, as needed.

1   pound unsalted butter, softened to room temperature
1   jalapeño pepper, seeded and minced
1   shallot, peeled and minced
½   bunch cilantro, finely chopped
1   tablespoon kosher salt
1   tablespoon freshly ground black pepper

Place all ingredients in a food processor. Blend until all are thoroughly incorporated.

PECAN-CRUSTED CHICKEN BREAST WITH RASPBERRY-CHIPOTLE CREAM

→→— SERVES 6 —←←

We created this nutty dish when we launched our catering business, Reata on the Road. After all, we were without a Fort Worth home for 15 months, so we had to have something to do! Our unplanned road show allowed us to expand our presence around Cowtown through hundreds of community and charity events, and today, we're one of the top caterers in the Fort Worth area. An entrée that's an exciting alternative to those boring rubber chicken dinners, the Raspberry-Chipotle Cream coupled with crunchy pecans adds just the right amount of gusto to any banquet. The cream also stands up well to beef, pork, or game.

6 (8-ounce) chicken breasts, pounded and butterflied
 Egg Wash (page 140)
3 cups all-purpose flour
4 cups Crushed Pecan Coating
 Kosher salt
 Freshly ground black pepper
3/4 cup oil, added to the pan about 1 tablespoon at a time

Preheat the oven to 350 degrees F. Dip each chicken breast in the Egg Wash, then dredge in the flour, coating thoroughly. Shake off excess flour. Then return each coated breast to the Egg Wash, remove, and allow the excess Egg Wash to drip back into the bowl.

In a separate bowl, season the Crushed Pecan Coating with salt and pepper. Liberally crust each coated chicken breast with the Crushed Pecan Coating.

Heat a large sauté pan with oil over medium-high heat. Add a crusted chicken breast to the hot sauté pan. Shake the pan gently to keep the chicken from sticking. Cook for about 2 to 3 minutes or until the crust turns golden brown. Take care not to burn the pecans! Turn the chicken and cook the other side, shaking the pan to keep the chicken from sticking. Repeat the process for all 6 chicken breasts. You may need to add oil occasionally throughout.

Coat a large baking sheet with a thin layer of olive oil. Reserve the fried chicken on a coated baking sheet. Finish the chicken in the pre-heated oven for about 5 to 7 minutes. Serve each chicken breast on a bed of 2 to 3 tablespoons of Raspberry-Chipotle Cream, and drizzle each with a little extra Cream on top.

Crushed Pecan Coating

MAKES 4 CUPS

2 cups pecans, shelled
2 cups Sourdough Croutons (page 130)

Combine ingredients in a food processor. Pulse until finely ground and blended well.

Raspberry-Chipotle Cream

MAKES 2 CUPS

- ½ cup red wine
- 1 cup fresh raspberries, or frozen
- ¾ cup sugar
- 1 teaspoon black peppercorns, whole
  Kosher salt
  Freshly ground black pepper
- 1 dried bay leaf
- 2 chipotle peppers, canned in adobo sauce
- 1 cup heavy cream

In a saucepan over high heat, heat the red wine and the raspberries for about 3 to 5 minutes. When the wine sauce begins to bubble, add 1 teaspoon of the sugar, the whole peppercorns, salt, and pepper, stirring constantly. When the sugar is dissolved, add the bay leaf and chipotle peppers. Continue to cook over high heat, stirring constantly, until the sauce comes to a rapid boil. Lower the heat and reduce the sauce by 50 percent. Remove from the heat, and let cool.

When the sauce is cooled, add to a blender or food processor, reserving the pan for later use. Purée the sauce. Add the heavy cream to the reserved pan. Slowly add the puréed sauce to the cream, stirring constantly, while cooking over medium-high heat. As soon as the sauce begins to boil, lower the heat to medium. Continue cooking until the sauce begins to thicken slightly. Remove from the heat and strain through a fine mesh strainer before serving.

PORK CHOPS WITH SPICED-PEAR RUM SAUCE

→ SERVES 6 ←

Two kinds of rum come together with fruity pears and spicy red pepper for a surprising sauce that really packs a punch! The Citrus Soak used for the pork chops is a great all-purpose marinade for a variety of meats, and it's also excellent for marinating artichokes. To maximize the flavor, we suggest you marinate the pork overnight.

12 (5-ounce) pork chops, center-cut
1 yellow onion
2 tablespoons Reata Grill Spice (page 138)
3 cups Spiced-Pear Rum Sauce

Heat the grill to hot. Slice the onion in half and spear with a fork at the rounded end. Run the flat side of the onion over the hot grate to lightly season the grill. Lightly dust both sides of each pork chop in the Reata Grill Spice. Place the chops directly onto the grill for about 4 to 5 minutes on each side.

The pork is done when it is firm to the touch and turns white in color. Carefully turn chops and cook to desired temperature. Top each serving with ½ cup of Spiced-Pear Rum Sauce.

Citrus Soak

MAKES 10 CUPS

4 cups pineapple juice
2 cups soy sauce
2 cups orange juice, preferably fresh squeezed
¼ cup fresh garlic, minced
½ cup fresh cilantro, finely chopped

1 tablespoon kosher salt
1 (3-inch) piece fresh ginger root, minced
2 dried bay leaves
1 tablespoon black peppercorns, whole
½ cup olive oil

Combine all the ingredients in a large, nonreactive baking dish. Place the pork chops in the dish and marinate overnight.

Spiced-Pear Rum Sauce

MAKES ABOUT 4 CUPS

¼ cup Captain Morgan's Spiced Rum
¼ cup Myers's Jamaican Dark Rum
4 cups light corn syrup
1 teaspoon ground cinnamon
1½ teaspoon red pepper flakes
3 ripe pears, cored, peeled, and quartered

In a large saucepan, combine both types of rum, light corn syrup, cinnamon, and red pepper flakes, and bring to a rapid boil. Reduce the heat and simmer for about 15 minutes. Add the pears, and continue simmering for an additional 5 minutes. Remove from the heat.

STACKED CHICKEN ENCHILADAS

→→ SERVES 6 ←←

Tomatillo Sauce is what gives this traditional Mexican dish a tongue-pleasing tang. A member of the tomato family, the much tarter tomatillos are about one to two inches wide, have a papery outer skin, and are used when they're still green. This easy Mexican casserole is perfect to make ahead of time and freeze for later. The Tomatillo Sauce is also a delicious topping with grilled chicken or fish.

Enchilada Assembly

2½ cups Tomatillo Sauce
1½ cups heavy cream
¼   cup oil, for sautéing
18 corn tortillas
4   cups Chicken Stuffing
3   cups Monterey Jack cheese, shredded
3   green onions, thinly sliced

Preheat the oven to 350 degrees F. In a bowl, whisk the Tomatillo Sauce and heavy cream together until thoroughly incorporated. In a sauté pan, heat oil to medium. Heat the corn tortillas, one at a time, for about 5 seconds on each side, just until they are pliable. Place the warm tortillas on a baking sheet covered with paper towels to drain.

Immerse 1 tortilla in the Tomatillo Sauce, coating both sides. Remove, shake off the excess sauce, and place in a large baking dish. Repeat with 5 more tortillas, until the bottom of the dish is covered with 6 sauce-coated tortillas. Add a layer of about 2 cups of the Chicken Stuffing, spreading evenly over the tortilla layer. Sprinkle about 1 cup of the shredded cheese atop the chicken layer. Place 6 more sauce-coated tortillas over the cheese layer.

Using the remainder of the Chicken Stuffing, evenly spread the meat over the second layer of tortillas. Sprinkle a second cup of cheese over the second chicken layer. Place the last 6 sauce-coated tortillas over the second cheese layer. Top with the remaining shredded cheese. Bake in the preheated oven for about 15 to 20 minutes, or until cheese on top begins to bubble and turn golden brown. Garnish with sliced green onions.

Chicken Stuffing

MAKES 4 CUPS

3   cups Shredded Chicken from the Grill (page 84)
2   roma tomatoes, diced
2   tablespoons Chipotle Cream (page 75)
¼   cup Tomatillo Sauce
¼   cup heavy cream
1   tablespoon fresh cilantro, finely chopped

In a large bowl, combine the chicken with the diced tomatoes. Add the Chipotle Cream to the chicken mixture and combine thoroughly. Add the Tomatillo Sauce and heavy cream, mixing well. Add the cilantro, mixing well. Reserve for the enchilada assembly.

Tomatillo Sauce

MAKES 4 CUPS

1¼   pound (about 10 to 12) tomatillos
7   garlic cloves, peeled
⅓   cup honey
½   yellow onion, diced
2   tablespoons fresh cilantro, roughly chopped
1   cup cold water

Preheat the oven to 350 degrees F. Place the tomatillos in a large stockpot, and cover with water, letting soak for 5 minutes. Peel the tomatillo husks. Place the peeled tomatillos on a baking sheet in the oven and bake for 15 minutes. Combine the garlic, honey, onions, cilantro, and water in a saucepan. Simmer over medium-high heat for 15 to 20 minutes. Remove from the heat and let cool completely. Pour into food processor or blender and purée.

PISTACHIO-CRUSTED TILAPIA

— SERVES 6 —

From nuts and seeds to cornmeal and chips, we coat and crust fish all the time in the restaurant. And if you're not a pistachio person, try pine nuts instead. The spices and honey-mustard paste listed below adapt well for most nuts, or you could use about 1½ cups stone-ground cornmeal. Mixing crushed blue and yellow tortilla chips also provides a tasty and colorful coating—all you have to do is bread the fish in the finely broken chips mixed with a little kosher salt and freshly ground black pepper before you sauté. Finally, there's a blackening option to kick your crust up a notch. Remember, if tilapia doesn't tip your hat, any flaky white fish works well for crusting.

1½   cup raw pistachios, shelled
1½   teaspoons dried oregano, crumbled
1½   teaspoons dried thyme, crumbled
¾   teaspoon garlic powder
6   (8-ounce) tilapia filets
    Kosher salt
    Freshly ground black pepper
5   tablespoons honey mustard
2   tablespoons olive oil

Combine the pistachios, oregano, thyme, and garlic powder in a food processor. Blend until finely chopped. Transfer to a shallow dish. Season both sides of tilapia with salt and pepper. In a bowl, combine the honey and mustard, and mix thoroughly. Brush a generous coating of the honey-mustard mixture over both sides of fish. Then dredge the coated tilapia in the crushed nut blend, pressing the crust firmly into each side of the fish.

In a large sauté pan, heat the oil over medium heat. Add the coated tilapia, cooking about 2 to 3 minutes per side, or until the fish is fork tender.

Variation

For a different type of blackening seasoning, try basting the filets in ½ cup melted butter instead of the honey-mustard. Then coat with the following:

¼   cup ground paprika
2   tablespoons ground thyme
2   teaspoons onion powder
1   teaspoon garlic powder
1   teaspoon kosher salt
¼   teaspoon ground red pepper

VENISON CHOPS WITH BERRY GOOD GAME SAUCE

Since it took so long to make that Veal Stock with the Port Wine Glaze, we've made our Berry Good Game Sauce nice and simple. The fresh blackberries offset the wild game with a sweet yet tangy complement. Because venison is so lean, we recommend cooking to a medium-rare temperature so the chops stay juicy and flavorful.

12 (4-ounce) venison chops
6 tablespoons unsalted butter, melted for basting
2 tablespoons Reata Grill Spice (page 138)
1½ cups Berry Good Game Sauce

Preheat the grill to high. Lightly dust both sides of each chop with the Reata Grill Spice. Place the chops directly on the grill, basting continuously with the melted butter, about 4 minutes. Overcooked venison gets really tough, so we're begging you to stop at medium-rare—and don't forget to baste, baste, baste while the chops are on the grill.

Carefully turn the chops, liberally basting with melted butter and cook, about 4 minutes, or until they reach the desired temperature.

Drizzle each serving with about 1 tablespoon of Berry Good Game Sauce, and garnish with a few cooked, whole blackberries from the sauce.

Berry Good Game Sauce

MAKES 1½ CUPS

1 cup Port Wine Glaze (page 94)
¼ cup brown sugar
1½ cups fresh blackberries
½ teaspoon freshly ground black pepper

Combine all the ingredients in a small saucepan over low heat. Simmer for about 20 to 30 minutes, taking care to not to break down the blackberries (though some will naturally occur).

DESSERTS

APPLE CRISP WITH CAJETA - 110
Crisp Topping
Cajeta

CHOCOLATE CHUNK BREAD PUDDING TAMALE WITH CRÈME ANGLAISE - 113
Crème Anglaise

CHOCOLATE MOUSSE - 114

CHIPOTLE BROWNIE - 115

DESSERT TACOS - 116
Taco Shells
Chocolate Ganache
Caramelized Bananas
Strawberries Sundance

**MOLTEN CHOCOLATE CAKE
WITH DRUNKEN BERRIES - 119**
Drunken Berries

BERRY CRÈME BRÛLÉE - 120

**WEST TEXAS PECAN PIE
WITH BOURBON CREAM - 125**
Bourbon Cream
Julie's Mom's Pie Crust

APPLE CRISP WITH CAJETA

Apple pie has certainly been around the campfire awhile. In fact, our twist on an American tradition really and truly can be made in a Dutch oven while you're hunting for wild game, or maybe just some peace and quiet. This long-time favorite is so popular at the Fort Worth restaurant we have to peel two cases of Granny Smiths every day! Some people say it's the Crisp Topping that calls their name, others drool over our Cajeta—a rich Mexican caramel made from goat's milk. The batch below makes plenty, so you can pour it on nice and thick. And if you're going for broke, add a scoop of your favorite vanilla ice cream, or serve atop a pool of our Bourbon Cream.

8 Granny Smith apples, peeled and cored
1 cup heavy cream
1 cup sugar
¼ cup all-purpose flour
1 tablespoon ground cinnamon
1 tablespoon lemon juice
½ teaspoon kosher salt
3 cups Crisp Topping
1 cup (at least) Cajeta

Preheat the oven to 350 degrees F. Butter a 9 by 13-inch baking pan and set it aside. Slice the apples into thin wedges. In a large bowl, toss the apple slices with the cream, sugar, flour, cinnamon, lemon juice, and salt. Layer the dressed apples in the prepared baking pan and generously spread the Crisp Topping over the apples. Bake for 45 to 60 minutes, or until the apples are soft and the mixture is bubbling. Drizzle with the Cajeta and serve warm.

Crisp Topping

ABOUT 3 CUPS

1½ cups flour
1 cup light brown sugar, packed
2 teaspoons ground cinnamon
¼ teaspoon kosher salt
12 tablespoons (¾ cup) unsalted butter

Combine the flour, brown sugar, cinnamon, and salt in a bowl. Cut the cold butter into small pieces and mix into the dry mixture with a fork, being careful not to overwork the mixture; it should appear crumbly.

Cajeta

MAKES 4 CUPS

4 cups sugar
1 cup water
¼ cup unsalted butter
1 to 2 cups heavy cream, or goat's milk

Combine the sugar and water in a large, heavy saucepan. Bring the mixture to a boil, stirring to dissolve the sugar. When the sugar is dissolved and the mixture begins to simmer, do not stir again.

Lower the heat and continue to cook at a slow, steady simmer for up to 30 minutes. The mixture will turn light brown in color; just as the mixture begins to turn darker brown and starts to thicken, slowly stir in the butter, then add the cream. The consistency should be thick like caramel, while remaining golden brown. The Cajeta will thicken as it cools, so this sauce is best served warm.

CHOCOLATE CHUNK BREAD PUDDING TAMALE WITH CRÈME ANGLAISE

—◆— SERVES 8 TO 10 —◆—

A traditional bread pudding provides a lovely finale when entertaining friends or family. But serving bread pudding in a tamale? The creative presentation behind an old favorite was Chef Juan Jamarillo's brilliant idea. For years, we've been taking the Buttermilk Pecan Biscuits from the previous day and using them for a classic bread pudding. You can do the same, and then you don't need to add pecans—unless you're just feeling extra nutty that day. But, if you haven't gotten around to making those biscuits yet, any hearty, dense bread that's stale and dry to the touch will do. One of the best things about these tamales is being able to make them ahead of time. Right before serving, just wrap the husks in a wet paper towel and reheat in the microwave.

8   to 10 corn husks
3   eggs
1   (14-ounce) can sweetened condensed milk
1   cup heavy cream
1/2   teaspoon pure vanilla extract
3   tablespoons unsalted butter, melted
1   teaspoon lemon juice
1   teaspoon kosher salt
1/2   cup chopped pecans
4   ounces semi-sweet baker's chocolate, chopped
6   cups (about 10 slices) roughly crumbled dry bread, or biscuits
2   cups Crème Anglaise (page 114)
2   cups Cajeta (page 110)

Soak the dried corn husks in hot water until pliable, usually about 1 to 2 hours. Preheat the oven to 300 degrees F. Butter an 8 by 8-inch baking pan and set it aside. In a large mixing bowl, beat the eggs. Add the milk and cream, and whisk to blend. Add the remaining ingredients, except the Crème Anglaise and Cajeta.

Toss to combine and pour into the prepared pan. Bake for 1 hour. The pudding is cooked when a knife inserted near the middle will come out moist but clean. Remove from the oven and let cool slightly.

On a clean, dry work surface, lay the husks flat. Place about 2 tablespoons of the warm bread pudding in the center of each husk, and spread it to within about 1 inch of the edge. Fold or tie each end. Just before serving, slice down the middle of each husk and generously top the bread pudding with both the Crème Anglaise and the Cajeta.

Variations

Substitute 1 1/2 cups raisins for the chocolate. Use Buttermilk-Pecan Biscuits (page 135), with or without pecans; if made with, omit the additional pecans.

continued

Crème Anglaise

SERVES 8, ABOUT 4 CUPS

- 2 sticks unsalted butter
- 2 cups sugar
- 1 quart heavy cream
- 1 egg
- 2 tablespoons vanilla

Melt the butter in a sauce pan until it begins to bubble. Whisk in the sugar, whisking constantly as the sugar dissolves. Slowly add the heavy cream, whisking constantly. Add the egg and vanilla. Lower the heat and continue cooking until the mixture is reduced by about 25 percent. Remove from the heat, and let cool slightly. Serve warm, but not hot. Cover and refrigerate for up to three days.

CHOCOLATE MOUSSE

→• SERVES 6 •←

A fantastic chocolate mousse recipe is absolutely essential for the home chef. Simple suppers become elegant evenings when they conclude with a whipped cloud of chocolate. Add a little Cajeta and some Crisp Topping before serving, and tell your guests you're adding some fiber to make it a little bit healthier for them!

- ¾ cup whole milk
- ½ cup sweetened condensed milk
- ½ cup Chocolate Ganache (page 118)
- 1 package (5.1 ounces) instant vanilla pudding
- 1½ cups heavy cream
- Chocolate shavings, for garnish
- Whipped cream, for garnish

Using an electric mixer, on the low setting, whisk together the whole milk, sweetened condensed milk, and Chocolate Ganache. Add the dry pudding, continuing to whisk so the powder combines with the chocolate, until thick and smooth. Place the pudding in an airtight container in the refrigerator to chill until firm, about 15 minutes. While the pudding is chilling, whip the heavy cream until stiff peaks form. After pudding has set, fold in the whipped cream. Refrigerate to chill another 30 minutes (at least) before serving.

CHIPOTLE BROWNIE

Juan Rodriguez, one of the spiciest members of our Fort Worth kitchen, came up with these brownies that literally radiate slow heat across your insides. The warmth of the pepper in these brownies makes that deep dark chocolate flavor last way longer than your last bite. The only thing that can make these brownies any better is a scoop of ice cream or an ice-cold glass of frothy milk.

4	eggs
1	cup brown sugar
1	cup granulated sugar
1¼	cup powdered cocoa, sifted
½	cup all-purpose flour
2	sticks unsalted butter, melted
1	teaspoon vanilla
½	teaspoon kosher salt
1	chipotle pepper, minced
2	tablespoons adobo sauce, canned
1	cup chopped pecans

Preheat the oven to 300 degrees F. Butter an 8 by 12-inch baking pan and set aside. Using an electric mixer, beat the eggs until light and fluffy. Add the sugar and brown sugar, continuing to mix. Add the remaining ingredients and continue mixing until all are well incorporated. Pour the mixture into the prepared baking pan, and bake for 1 hour. Remove from the oven and let cool before slicing and serving.

DESSERT TACOS

Candy-like taco shells are what turns simple ice cream into a Mexican sundae. I recommend purchasing a ¾ to 1-inch wooden (preferably hardwood) dowel for forming the shells, and make sure it's clean prior to using it. It's also important that your baking sheet is completely flat (we know sometimes the heat of the oven can make thin ones warp or buckle after they've been around awhile). We serve our Dessert Tacos with Caramelized Bananas, some fresh strawberries, white chocolate shavings, and fresh mint. Here's a secret: If you're not crazy about bananas, then consider topping your taco with Strawberries Sundance instead. Shouldn't sundaes be all about what makes you happy anyway?

Taco Shells

4	tablespoons unsalted butter
½	cup brown sugar
2	tablespoons light corn syrup
¼	teaspoon vanilla
½	cup all-purpose flour

Preheat the oven to 350 degrees F. Prepare a cookie sheet with nonstick baking spray and set aside.

In a saucepan, melt the butter over medium heat. Add the brown sugar, stirring constantly. Stir in the corn syrup and vanilla, cook for 5 minutes, stirring constantly. Slowly stir in the flour until mixed well. Remove from the heat.

Using a metal spatula, spread the mixture over the prepared cookie sheet to an even thickness of ¼ inch. Bake in the preheated oven for 5 minutes until the mixture bubbles vigorously, turns darker in color, and spreads even more. Remove from the oven, and let cool for 1 hour.

Reheat the mixture, on the same cookie sheet, in a 350-degree oven, until it barely begins to soften, about 2 to 3 minutes. Remove from the oven. Using a biscuit cutter, cut circles into the mixture. Using a spatula or pie server, carefully remove each circle while still pliable, and drape over the dowel to cool.

Assembling the Tacos

PER SERVING, 2 TACOS EACH

¼	cup Chocolate Ganache (page 118)
	Vanilla ice cream
2	tablespoons Caramelized Bananas or Strawberries Sundance (page 118)
1	tablespoon strawberries, chopped
1	tablespoon white chocolate, shaved
	Fresh mint, julienned for garnish

Ladle the Chocolate Ganache onto a dessert plate. Gently fill 1 taco shell with 2 tablespoons of the ice cream. Place the filled shell in the bed of Chocolate Ganache. (When heated, the consistency of the Ganache is quite pourable; as it cools to room temperature, it thickens considerably and will hold the tacos securely enough to keep them from sliding around the plate.) Top with 1 tablespoon of the Caramelized Bananas or Strawberries Sundance. Add about ½ tablespoon of strawberries to the taco. Garnish with about ½ tablespoon of the white chocolate

continued

shavings and mint. Repeat with the second taco to complete 1 serving.

Chocolate Ganache

MAKES 2½ CUPS

Our fudgy ganache makes a perfect bed to cradle the Dessert Tacos, but it's also excellent as a topper for many of our other desserts, including the Chocolate Mousse.

  1   cup heavy cream
 ³/₄ cup sugar
  1   stick unsalted butter
 ¹/₄ cup light corn syrup
 ¹/₂ pound bittersweet chocolate, chopped

Heat the cream, sugar, butter, and corn syrup in a saucepan over medium heat, stirring constantly so it doesn't burn. Add the chocolate, and continue to stir until all the ingredients are melted and incorporated.

Caramelized Bananas

MAKES 3 CUPS

 ³/₄ cup packed brown sugar
 ³/₄ cup cold unsalted butter, cut into pieces
  4   bananas, diced

Heat the brown sugar in a saucepan over medium heat. When the sugar starts to melt, add the butter and whisk to blend. When the mixture becomes liquid and very hot, add the bananas all at once. Stir to coat the bananas with syrup. Remove from the heat and let cool.

Strawberries Sundance

MAKES 3 TO 4 CUPS

A perfect light dessert all on their own, these strawberries are dreamy with a drizzle of Bourbon Cream. Allow them to chill overnight, or at least an hour or two, to maximize the flavors.

 1¹/₂ pints (about 2 pounds) fresh strawberries, quartered
 ¹/₄ cup brown sugar
  2   tablespoons orange juice
  2   teaspoons vanilla extract
 ¹/₄ cup light corn syrup
  2   teaspoons cinnamon
  2   teaspoons orange liqueur

Combine all the ingredients in large bowl, mixing well to ensure that all the strawberries are coated and that the sugar is dissolved. Cover and refrigerate overnight.

MOLTEN CHOCOLATE CAKE WITH DRUNKEN BERRIES

—◆— Serves 6 to 8 —◆—

To get the true "molten" effect, these really must be made in individual foil tins. We've included some suggested baking times for a few standard containers. But the most important thing you need to know is that when a slight crust begins to develop on the top of the cake, this baby is done baking. Like a volcano, it's supposed to ooze warm and gooey fudge from the center, so please don't bake any longer—take them out of the oven when we say so—and you'll be glad you did!

6   eggs
½   cup granulated sugar
½   pound semi-sweet baker's chocolate, chopped
2   sticks butter, cut into small squares
⅓   cup heavy cream
1   tablespoon vanilla
½   cup all-purpose flour
    Crème Anglaise (page 114), for garnish
    Drunken Berries, for garnish
    Fresh mint, for garnish
    Powdered sugar, for garnish

Using an electric mixer, mix the eggs and sugar on high, until the mixture forms a soft and ribbon-like meringue. Set aside. In a small saucepan, combine the chocolate, butter, and cream over medium heat, stirring often, until melted. Very gently and carefully fold in the meringue mixture. Add the vanilla and gently mix, taking care not to break down the meringue. Sift the flour into the batter, and carefully mix. Chill in an airtight container in the refrigerator for 1 hour.

Preheat the oven to 350 degrees F. Coat 6 to 8 foil cups (4 ounces each) with nonstick baking spray and granulated sugar. Pour approximately ½ cup of the batter into each foil cup filling to about ¼ inch from the top of the cup. Place the foil cups on a cookie sheet and bake in the preheated oven for about 17 minutes. Remove from the oven. Remove the cakes from the cookie sheet, and let cool on cooling rack for 30 minutes. Gently turn each cup upside down and let the cakes gently release themselves from the foil cups.

Pour ¼ cup of Crème Anglaise onto a dessert plate. Place the cake in the center of the cream. Top with about ¼ cup of Drunken Berries (with the juice). Garnish with a spring of fresh mint, and dust with powdered sugar.

Suggested Baking Times for Foil Tins

2.5-ounce containers, bake 13 minutes
4-ounce containers, bake 17 minutes

Drunken Berries
MAKES ABOUT 1½ CUPS

2   cups mixed fresh berries (raspberries, strawberries, blackberries, and/or blueberries), or frozen
¼   cup granulated sugar
¼   cup white wine

Mix all the ingredients together in a bowl. Place in an airtight container in the refrigerator. Chill until frozen berries have thawed and/or made their own juice. If using fresh berries, chill at least 2 hours, but 6 hours would be even better.

BERRY CRÈME BRÛLÉE

Crème Brûlée may seem fancy to some folks, but the truth is the warm custard is really not that hard to make. Just be methodical and take it slow when you "temper" the warm vanilla cream into the egg and sugar mixture. Tempering means to slowly bring up the temperature of an ingredient by adding small amounts of a hot liquid. By adding the vanilla cream gradually and stirring it constantly, you will keep from inadvertently scrambling your eggs—which are fantastic for breakfast, but not for Crème Brûlée!

1 pint blackberries
11 egg yolks
1¼ cups granulated sugar
1 quart heavy cream
1 tablespoon vanilla
½ cup granulated sugar, for topping

Preheat the oven to 250 degrees F. Place 3 to 5 blackberries in the bottom of each of 6 individual ramekins, or small oven-safe serving bowls, and set aside. In a large mixing bowl, whisk together the egg yolks and sugar. In a saucepan, combine the cream and the vanilla, and heat to approximately 160 degrees F, stirring constantly to prevent burning. Slowly temper the warm vanilla cream into the egg and sugar mixture, stirring constantly. Skim the foam off the top of the mixture.

Ladle about 1 cup of the mixture into each serving bowl. Place all the bowls into braising pan, or baking dish that is deep enough to hold the bowls and the water. Fill the braising pan with water to halfway up the serving bowls. Bake for about 75 minutes. The custard is done when an inserted toothpick comes out clean. Remove from the oven and the water bath, and let cool slightly.

Sprinkle each serving with sugar. Using a butane torch, slowly and evenly brown the sugar topping, taking care to only caramelize and not scorch. If you don't have a butane torch, you can place the sugar-topped custards under the broiler very briefly. Watch very closely, as the sugar will turn dark very quickly.

Variations

Substitute raspberries or blueberries for blackberries.

Subsitute ¼ cup Chocolate Ganache (page 118) for the fruit.

WEST TEXAS PECAN PIE WITH BOURBON CREAM

→ SERVES 6 TO 8 →

Every southern cook should have a bottle of Karo syrup in the pantry. Seems this thick, sweet staple is a big help around the whole house, not just the kitchen. We know one new momma who used it to stick cute little bows atop her bald baby's head! But she's holding off on the Bourbon Cream until her little one comes of age.

3 eggs
1 teaspoon vanilla
¼ cup granulated sugar
¼ teaspoon kosher salt
1 cup Karo Dark Corn Syrup
1 cup pecans, shelled and halved
Julie's Mom's Pie Crust (page 126)

Preheat the oven to 350 degrees F. Lightly whisk the eggs with the vanilla and sugar. Add the salt and corn syrup, and whisk well. Pour into an unbaked pie crust. Gently add the pecans so they float evenly across the top of the liquid mixture. Bake in the preheated oven for 30 minutes. Remove from the oven, and let cool at least 30 minutes to set.

Serve each slice nestled in a pool of warm Bourbon Cream.

Bourbon Cream

MAKES 2 CUPS

½ cup unsalted butter
½ cup granulated sugar
1 cup heavy cream
⅓ cup bourbon whiskey, your preferred variety

Melt the butter over medium heat in a saucepan. Slowly add the sugar, stirring with a wooden spoon, and cook for about 3 minutes, or until the sugar dissolves. The mixture will be opaque, not clear. Add the cream and the bourbon, stirring constantly. Continue cooking to about 180 degrees F. Use a candy thermometer to check the temperature, remembering not to touch the bottom of the pan. Let the mixture simmer for 5 minutes, and remove from the heat. Serve immediately.

continued

Julie's Mom's Pie Crust

MAKES 2 PIE CRUSTS

It may have been hard to spell her name (Taini is an Indian name, pronounced "Tina"), but it sure wasn't hard to learn how to cook from Julie's mom. This one-time military wife turned single mother improvised and made-do in the kitchen with a wealth of natural talent and insisted that her daughters develop their culinary skills early. So Julie and her sister Erin perfected Taini's homemade pie crust with dough scraps, butter, cinnamon, and sugar all carefully smashed into a tiny pan from their toy Easy-Bake Oven, and their miniature crust was baked right smack alongside the grown-up pie in the big oven. Taini's baking pies for the angels now—and Julie's certain they get the cinnamon-crust treats on the side, just like she did when she was six years old.

3	cups flour
1½	teaspoon salt
1½	cup shortening
1	egg
5	tablespoons ice-cold 7–Up, or club soda
1	tablespoon white vinegar

Mix the flour, salt, and shortening until the mixture resembles coarse crumbs. Combine egg, soda, and vinegar. Stir the wet ingredients into the flour mixture quickly to form dough that clings together and "cleans" the bowl. Work the dough into a smooth, flat round. Roll out to about ⅛ inch thick, using liberal amounts of flour.

If another recipe calls for a baked shell (the West Texas Pecan Pie doesn't), bake the empty shell for about 15 to 20 minutes in the oven pre-heated to 350 degrees F. The crust is done when it turns golden brown.

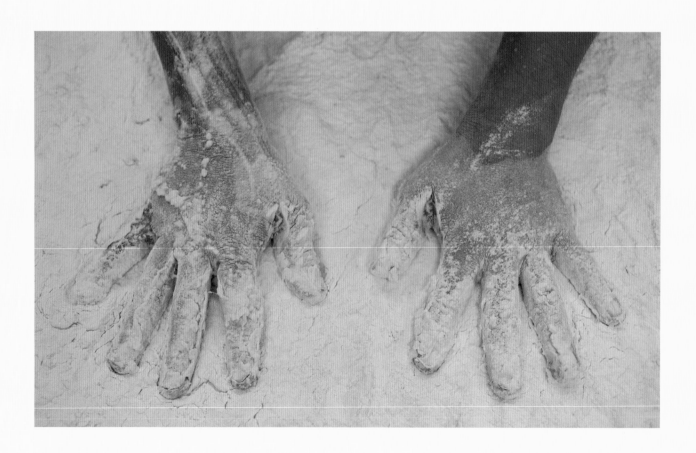

EXTRAS

24-HOUR SOURDOUGH BISCUITS - 130
24-Hour Sourdough Starter
Sourdough Croutons

BARBECUE SAUCE - 132
Bourbon Barbecue Sauce

ROASTED SHALLOTS - 132

APPLE JACK CHUNK - 133

AVOCADO-LIME CREAM SAUCE - 133

BUTTERMILK-PECAN BISCUITS - 135

CUCUMBER PICO - 135

ORANGE-SESAME DRESSING - 136

REATA BLACKENING SEASONING - 136

HORSERADISH SOUR CREAM - 137

MANGO RELISH - 137

REATA CHICKEN RUB - 138

REATA FLOUR SPICE - 138

REATA GRILL SPICE - 138

REATA PICKLES - 140

EGG WASH - 140

SALSA ROJO - 141

ROASTED GARLIC - 141

SIERRA LA RANA CORN MUFFINS - 142

TEQUILA CREAM SAUCE - 144

DILL-HORSERADISH CREAM - 144

VEAL STOCK - 145

24-HOUR SOURDOUGH BISCUITS

Sourdough has been a staple since the cattle drives. It tastes swell, but honestly, who today has the time (or the room in their refrigerator!) to feed that starter every day, over and over and over? So we came up with a great alternative: the 24-Hour Sourdough Starter. Simply make it the day before you want the biscuits. We think they come out about perfect when you bake them in a well-seasoned cast-iron skillet. The croutons add the perfect crunch to any salad or stew. And it's totally fine to down a handful or two from time to time.

24-Hour Sourdough Starter

- 2 cups all-purpose flour
- 1½ cups water, warm
- 2 tablespoons plain full-fat yogurt
- 2 teaspoons (1 packet) yeast, dry and active

Combine all the ingredients in a large mixing bowl. Cover loosely with tin foil and let sit at room temperature for 24 hours. You really do need a large bowl for this step, as the starter will bubble and ferment overnight, substantially growing in size. However, after about 24 hours, it will settle down and return to close to its original size.

24-Hour Sourdough Biscuits

- 24-Hour Sourdough Starter
- 2½ cups all-purpose flour
- 2 teaspoons baking powder
- 1 teaspoon iodized salt
- 2 tablespoons sugar
- Flour for rolling surface
- 4 tablespoons unsalted butter, cold and cubed

Generously butter an 8 to 10-inch, well-seasoned cast-iron skillet. In a large bowl, thoroughly combine the 24-Hour Sourdough Starter with the flour, baking powder, salt, and sugar. Liberally flour a clean, dry work surface. Place the dough on the flour-coated work surface, kneading it several times, until it is smooth and pliable. Carefully fold in the butter, being careful not to overknead the dough. The texture of the dough should be soft and smooth—not too sticky but not too dry.

Pinch off dough balls about the size of a lemon, nestling the balls right next to each other in the skillet. Cover and let rise, at room temperature, for 30 minutes. Preheat the oven to 350 degrees F. Bake for 45 minutes.

Sourdough Croutons

- Leftover Sourdough Biscuits (a day or two old is fine, if still soft enough to easily cut)
- Per roll, 1 to 2 tablespoons unsalted butter, melted

Preheat the oven to 350 degrees F. Cut the bread into 2-inch chunks and place in a large bowl. Add the melted butter and mix until the bread is softened but not wet, being careful not to crush the bread chunks. Spread the coated bread pieces in a baking pan, leaving a little room between the pieces so they don't stick together while baking. Bake for about 15 to 20 minutes, depending on how crispy you like your croutons.

BARBECUE SAUCE

In Texas, the ingredients in your barbecue sauce are almost as personal as what's in your medicine cabinet. In fact, our state has whole contests and festivals dedicated to barbecue tastings. You can use this sauce as is, or try it as a base and then doctor it up yourself. Our team of chefs recently got competitive in the kitchen, and this is the sauce that came out on top.

1½ cups ketchup
⅓ cup tomato paste
¾ cup Worcestershire sauce
1½ tablespoons allspice
1 tablespoon dried ground mustard
½ teaspoon cayenne pepper
⅓ cup white wine vinegar
¼ cup fresh lemon juice
1½ tablespoons garlic powder
¾ cup brown sugar
¼ cup sugar
2 cups water
¼ teaspoon kosher salt
1½ tablespoons freshly ground black pepper

Combine all the ingredients in a saucepan. Cook slowly over low heat for about 2 hours. Remove from the heat, and let cool. Serve at room temperature. Cover, and refrigerate for up to three days.

Bourbon Barbecue Sauce

2 cups Barbecue Sauce
¼ cup brown sugar
½ cup bourbon whiskey, your favorite variety

Combine all the ingredients in a saucepan, and cook slowly over low heat for 1 hour. Remove from the heat, and let cool. Serve at room temperature. Cover, and refrigerate for up to three days.

ROASTED SHALLOTS

3 shallots, peeled
2 tablespoons extra virgin olive oil

Preheat the oven to 300 degrees F. Place the shallots in a braising pan and coat with the oil. Tightly cover pan with foil. Bake for 30 to 45 minutes, or until the shallots are aromatic and soft. Remove from oven and let cool thoroughly. Store in an airtight container in the refrigerator.

APPLE JACK CHUNK

This tangy yet sweet chutney is exceptional when paired with grilled pork chops or chicken. We think of it as an adult applesauce. Our favorite bourbon is Jack Daniels, but we're all about you picking your own pleasure.

1	cup brown sugar
1/2	cup bourbon whiskey, your favorite variety
2	Granny Smith apples, cored, peeled, and diced
1	yellow onion, diced
1	red onion, diced
2	stalks celery, diced

Heat a large sauté pan over medium-high heat. Combine all the ingredients in the preheated pan, stirring frequently. Sauté until the mixture is reduced by about 50 percent and the sauce is thick and syrup-like. Serve warm. Cover, and refrigerate for up to three days.

AVOCADO-LIME CREAM SAUCE

Even though we are known for our beef, our daily fish special is always a hit. Avocado and lime are generally items used in lighter salsas, so your mouth gets a nice surprise when you taste the citrus paired with rich cream and buttery avocado. We especially like to serve this in the winter atop a flaky white fish.

	Juice of 3 limes
2	tablespoons white wine
1/2	teaspoon Tabasco sauce
1/2	teaspoon black peppercorns, whole
1	dried bay leaf
1	quart heavy cream
1	teaspoon fresh cilantro, finely chopped
2	avocados, diced large
	Kosher salt
	Freshly ground black pepper

Combine the lime juice, white wine, Tabasco, peppercorns, and bay leaf in a saucepan and cook over high heat, bringing the mixture to a boil. Reduce the liquid by 50 percent, then lower the heat. Slowly add the heavy cream, stirring constantly, and bring the mixture back to a boil. Reduce the cream sauce by about 50 percent. Remove from the heat and let cool. When the sauce is cool, pour through a fine mesh strainer into a blender or food processor. Add the cilantro and the avocados and purée until smooth. Season with salt and pepper. Let cool, and serve at room temperature. Cover, and refrigerate for up to three days.

BUTTERMILK-PECAN BISCUITS

Our mouthwatering biscuits are served every day before every meal in both restaurants. And from time to time, we just know that a few of our regulars sneak some home in their purses to heat up for later. That's okay—we don't mind a bit. After all, when you heat up a little leftover tenderloin, or better yet, a CF Steak, and serve these under a boatload of our Cracked-Pepper Cream Gravy, well, there's simply nothing better for breakfast.

8	cups self-rising flour
2	cups pecans, coarsely chopped
3½	cups buttermilk
⅓	cup all-purpose flour
1	tablespoon unsalted butter, melted

In a large bowl, thoroughly combine all the ingredients. Liberally flour a clean, dry work surface. Knead the dough several more times until it is elastic, but not too sticky. Roll the dough to about ¾- to 1-inch thick. With a large knife, score the dough into 2-inch squares, being careful not to cut the dough all the way through. Place the scored dough on a baking sheet in one piece, then carefully slice through scores to make clean cuts. Let the biscuits rise on the baking sheet for about 1 hour.

Preheat the oven to 350 degrees F. Bake for about 30 to 35 minutes. The biscuits are done when the tops are golden brown. For some extra flavor, brush the tops with melted butter just before serving.

CUCUMBER PICO

This is the perfect pico de gallo for late summer suppers outdoors. You can top your grilled fish with this garden-fresh salsa, or just scoop it up with chips for an easy, light appetizer.

1	cucumber, peeled, seeded, and diced
½	red onion, diced
7	green onions, thinly sliced
¾	cup red bell pepper, diced
7	green onions, thinly sliced
¼	cup white wine vinegar
¼	cup olive oil
2	tablespoons sugar

Kosher salt
Freshly ground black pepper

Combine all the ingredients in a large mixing bowl and blend well. Season with salt and pepper. Cover and chill for at least 3 to 4 hours before serving.

ORANGE-SESAME DRESSING

An excellent dressing for fresh spinach or crunchy romaine, the nutty citrus flavor also makes this a fine dipping sauce for our Braised Boar Ribs.

1/3	cup orange marmalade
1/2	teaspoon ancho chili powder
1/4	teaspoon garlic powder
1/4	cup white wine vinegar
2/3	cup extra virgin olive oil
2	tablespoons soy sauce
3	tablespoons sesame oil
2	tablespoons honey
1/2	cup mandarin orange slices, canned
1	tablespoon sesame seeds

Place all the ingredients, except the orange slices and sesame seeds, in a blender and mix until combined well. Transfer the dressing to an airtight container and add the oranges and sesame seeds. Shake vigorously and serve immediately, or refrigerate in an airtight container and shake well before serving.

REATA BLACKENING SEASONING

Contrary to popular belief, blackened doesn't mean burned! This flavorful spice combination gives that just-right charcoal taste, without that just-wrong charbroiled grit.

3	tablespoons ground paprika
1/2	tablespoon kosher salt
1	tablespoon onion powder
1	tablespoon garlic powder
1	tablespoon cayenne pepper
2 1/4	teaspoons freshly ground white pepper
1 1/2	teaspoons freshly ground black pepper
1 1/2	teaspoons ground dried thyme
1 1/2	teaspoons dried oregano, crumbled

Mix all the ingredients together, and store in an airtight container.

HORSERADISH SOUR CREAM

Zesty horseradish yearns for something cool and creamy, especially when you want to bring out the smoky flavors of a great cut of meat. Try a dollop on a leftover prime rib sandwich or a dab atop roasted pork tenderloin. If you must get all healthy on us, you can show off and use it as a dip for crunchy, fresh vegetables.

2½ cups sour cream

½ cup fresh horseradish, finely grated

1 tablespoon ground paprika

¾ teaspoon kosher salt

Combine all the ingredients in a bowl, and whisk vigorously until blended thoroughly. Serve immediately. Cover, and refrigerate for up to three days.

MANGO RELISH

Ripe mangos have a fragrant, fruity odor at the stem and feel firm yet yield to slight finger pressure. They ripen best at room temperature, but you can also place the fruit in a paper bag overnight to speed up the process. To cut a mango, peel it carefully and then slice off one side. Rotate the fruit so it's sitting on its flattest surface. Cut the remaining three sides off and slice the flesh into thin strips. Our relish pairs sweet mango with tangy cilantro and spicy jalapeños, and is perfect atop grilled fish.

4 fresh mangos, peeled and diced

⅓ cup red onion, diced

¼ cup red bell pepper, seeded and diced

1 jalapeño pepper, seeded and minced

1 teaspoon fresh cilantro, roughly chopped

2 teaspoons apple cider vinegar

2 teaspoons honey

Kosher salt

Coarsely ground black pepper

Combine all the ingredients in a large mixing bowl and blend well. Season with salt and pepper. Chill at least 3 to 4 hours before serving.

REATA CHICKEN RUB

⟿ MAKES 2 CUPS ⟾

Chicken always tastes better and has a nicer texture when cooked in its skin. Our rub is perfect to break through that layer of fat, allowing the flavors to penetrate throughout the meat for juicier chicken.

$1/4$ cup ground paprika
$1/4$ cup cayenne pepper
2 tablespoons ground coriander
2 tablespoons ground cumin
2 tablespoons freshly ground black pepper

2 teaspoons sugar
$2/3$ cup dark chili powder

Mix all the ingredients together, and store in an airtight container.

REATA FLOUR SPICE

⟿ MAKES $3^{1}/_{2}$ CUPS ⟾

Because one or both of these recipes are used in so many of our menu items (we go through 50-pound batches every week), we recommend you prepare some of each ahead of time and keep them on hand in an airtight container in a cool, dark place. A small bottle also makes a thoughtful gift for your favorite party host.

3 cups all-purpose flour
3 tablespoons iodized salt
4 tablespoons coarsely ground black pepper

Mix all the ingredients together, and store in an airtight container.

REATA GRILL SPICE

⟿ MAKES ABOUT $1^{1}/_{2}$ CUPS ⟾

$1/4$ cup freshly ground black pepper
2 tablespoons kosher salt
4 tablespoons ground thyme
3 tablespoons garlic
$2^{1}/_{2}$ tablespoons sugar

$1/4$ cup ground cumin
$1/2$ cup ground paprika

Mix all the ingredients together, and store in an airtight container.

REATA PICKLES

Our traditional pickles have the perfect pucker for either of our Tartar Sauce recipes. You might also want to experiment with fresh jalapeño peppers, baby carrots, or petite onions. Just omit the dried dill when pickling other items.

3 cloves fresh garlic, peeled
1 teaspoon yellow mustard seeds
1/4 teaspoon allspice
1/4 teaspoon ground cloves
2 dried bay leaves
1/4 teaspoon ground turmeric
1 teaspoon brown sugar
1 quart apple cider vinegar
3 tablespoons dried dill
1 teaspoon black peppercorns, whole
1 teaspoon kosher salt
1/4 cup white wine
1/2 yellow onion, diced
2 cucumbers, cut into 1/4-inch-thick slices, with the peel

Place all the ingredients, except cucumbers, in a large stockpot over medium-high heat and bring to a rapid boil. Remove from the heat and add the cucumbers to the stockpot, making sure they are completely covered with the liquid. Weight down the cucumbers by placing a round plate, slightly smaller than the circumference of the pot, over the cucumbers to ensure they remain submerged. Refrigerate at least 24 hours to ensure the cucumbers absorb all the flavors from the liquid. Drain off excess pickling liquid, while keeping a small reserve. Add the pickles and reserved liquid to a covered container, and refrigerate.

EGG WASH

One batch of egg wash is plenty for any of the recipes that call for it. This is a constant in our kitchen; we use it for everything we batter and fry. Because it will only keep a short while (about an hour), we recommend you make a batch right before you start cooking.

2 eggs
1 quart buttermilk

Break the eggs into a stainless steel bowl, and whisk until smooth. Add the buttermilk and whisk vigorously. If not using immediately, refrigerate at once.

SALSA ROJO

MAKES ABOUT 6 CUPS

We're pretty sure that native Texans are born with a thicker stomach lining than most anyone else. This has been helpful for keeping down hotter-than-fire salsa every day for the last eighty or so years. We eat salsa on everything, including our eggs at breakfast. But the truth of the matter is we know there's a lot of salsa sissies out there, so our Salsa Rojo has a medium amount of heat. If you're into doubling over after you eat, just beef up the jalapeños.

5   fresh tomatoes, roasted and diced
1   yellow onion, chopped
6   to 8 cloves fresh garlic, peeled
2   fresh lemons, squeezed for the juice
1   bunch fresh cilantro, coarsely chopped
2   jalapeño peppers, seeded and quartered
    Kosher salt
    Freshly ground black pepper

Heat the grill to medium and roast the whole tomatoes. When the skins begin to look soft and start to separate from the tomato flesh, remove from the heat and set aside to cool. Dice the tomatoes when cool to the touch. Place all the ingredients in a food processor, and pulse repeatedly until all are fully incorporated. Store in an airtight container in the refrigerator.

ROASTED GARLIC

MAKES 3 HEADS

Roasting brings out warm, rich flavors that will penetrate and enhance just about anything. You'll be surprised how often you reach for these surprisingly subtle, roasted additions to your favorite recipes.

3   whole garlic heads
3   teaspoons extra virgin olive oil
1/4   cup fresh thyme, stemmed and chopped

Preheat the oven to 350 degrees F. Peel away any excess outer skin from the garlic and slice a thin layer off the top to expose the individual cloves. Place the garlic in a small baking dish or on a piece of foil. Drizzle each head with oil and sprinkle with thyme. Tightly cover the garlic in foil and bake for 45 minutes to 1 hour, or until the garlic is aromatic and soft. Remove from the oven and let cool.

When the garlic has cooled slightly, gently squeeze the cloves out of their casings and mash with a fork, or purée in a food processor or blender. Store in an airtight container in the refrigerator.

SIERRA LA RANA CORN MUFFINS

When the weather gets crisp and cool, we love to make a big batch of these with any one of our soups or stews and curl up down home at the ranch. It's the Pico de Gallo that gives them a special twist. This name comes from our property just outside of Big Bend National Park called Sierra la Rana—a pristine 11,600-acre ranch community where you'll find more species of wildlife and plants than anywhere else in the Southwest, and you can gaze on some of the prettiest stars you've ever seen in those wide-open velvet skies.

2 cups dry cornmeal

2 cups all-purpose flour

2 cups fresh buttermilk

8 teaspoons baking powder

2 eggs

1/2 cup unsalted butter, melted

1/2 cup sugar

1 cup Pico de Gallo (page 55)

Preheat the oven to 350 degrees F. Butter mini-muffin tins, or use a well-seasoned cast-iron skillet or corn cake pan. Using an electric mixer, combine all the ingredients well to form a batter. Pour into the muffin tins and bake until the tops begin to turn golden brown, about 15 minutes. If baking in a skillet or pan, the corn cake is done when golden brown with some crust cracks across the top.

TEQUILA CREAM SAUCE

Lots of our sauces start by deglazing a pan. With this one, you'll deglaze the browned jalapeño and garlic. When deglazing with alcohol, it's really important to remove the sauté pan from the heat *before* adding the liquor or wine—otherwise, you might show up to the table without any eyebrows. When the pan is removed from the heat, add the tequila and start stirring. Our favorite tequila is Patron Silver; but really, just choose the brand you have on hand, or the one you're least likely to want for your margarita later.

4 tablespoons unsalted butter
6 to 8 jalapeño peppers, seeded and minced
2 tablespoons fresh garlic, minced
1 cup tequila, your favorite variety
Juice of 5 lemons
1¾ cups heavy cream
¼ cup honey
2 teaspoons capers

In a small saucepan, sauté the jalapeños and garlic in butter over medium heat. Deglaze the pan with tequila and lemon juice. Turn heat to low and reduce the liquid by about 25 percent, just long enough to cook off the alcohol from the tequila, but leaving the flavor. Very slowly whisk in the cream, stirring constantly, so the butter doesn't separate from the cream. Add the honey and capers. Continue cooking over low heat and reduce by at least 50 percent. Serve immediately. Cover and refrigerate for up to three days.

DILL-HORSERADISH CREAM

Another one of our best-selling fish specials is grilled or pan-seared salmon topped with this zesty cream sauce. The fresh horseradish is just right to give the salmon a special little kick in the gills.

5 slices bacon, diced
1 red onion, diced
2 tablespoons fresh horseradish, finely grated
¼ cup white wine
1 quart heavy cream
¼ cup fresh dill, roughly chopped

In a large sauté pan over medium-high heat, cook the diced bacon until crisp. When the bacon is cooked, add the red onion and horse-radish and sauté for about 3 minutes, or until the onion is soft and translucent. Deglaze pan with white wine and cook for about 2 more minutes. Lower the heat to medium and slowly add the heavy cream, stirring constantly so it doesn't scorch. Let mixture reduce by about 25 percent, stirring often. Add the dill and cook for another 2 minutes. Remove from the heat and serve immediately. Cover, and refrigerate for up to three days.

VEAL STOCK

We'll 'fess up: This takes a long time to cook—but we swear it's not that hard. It's just not always practical to make it before you prepare a big meal, where maybe only one recipe calls for Veal Stock. So, if you must, you can combine equal parts of chicken stock and beef stock and get a flavor that's pretty close. But promise us you'll try this one day, okay? We promise it will be worth your while!

10 pounds veal bones
3 yellow onions, chopped
2 stalks celery, chopped
1 head fresh garlic, cloves peeled
¼ cup fresh thyme, diced
5 dried bay leaves
½ cup tomato paste
2 gallons water

Preheat the oven to 325 degrees F. Place the bones in a large, dry, covered roasting pan and cook for 3 hours. Add the water—be very careful, as the pan will be extremely hot and the water might spatter! Add all the remaining ingredients, cover, and roast for 1 hour. Remove from the oven. Carefully pour everything, including the bones, into a large stockpot. Cover, and cook over medium heat for at least 12 hours.

DRINKS

ALPINE ICED TEA

➤— SERVES 1 —➤

We Texans love our iced tea, sweet or not. And when we're ready to take a load off at the end of the day, our doctored-up tea does the deed real good. Of course, real Texans wouldn't be caught dead drinking anything developed by Yankees. Our smooth Alpine Iced Tea won't knock your boots off like that brash version from Long Island does.

1¼   ounces orange vodka
¾   ounce raspberry liqueur
¾   ounce melon liqueur
2   ounces pineapple juice
2   ounces cranberry juice
    Ice cubes
    Lemon wedge, for garnish

Combine all the ingredients in a drink shaker, and shake gently twice. Pour over ice cubes, and garnish with the lemon wedge.

BILLIONAIRE MARGARITA

➤— SERVES 1 —➤

These days, fifty bucks will just about fill up your tank, and we're not only talking gasoline here. You see, Reata's got a $50 margarita that's the best darn indulgence this side of the oil fields. Please don't wait until your well becomes a gusher before you try it. Sometimes just making it to the end of a long hard day is enough of a victory to splurge on this first-class cocktail.

1¼   ounces Don Julio 1942 Anejo tequila
¾   ounce Grand Marnier 150th Anniversary liqueur
3   ounces lime juice, preferably fresh squeezed
2   teaspoons sugar
    Salt, to coat rim of glass
    Ice cubes
    Lime wedge, for garnish

Combine all the ingredients in a drink shaker, and shake gently twice. Rim a glass with the salt and add ice cubes. Pour over ice, and garnish with the lime wedge.

BIRTHDAY CAKE COCKTAIL

⟶ SERVES 1 ⟵

Our Birthday Cake Cocktail was concocted for our 10th anniversary celebration of Reata Fort Worth in May 2006, and honestly, it tastes just like that grocery-store white cake with whipped icing we all had at childhood birthday parties. Here's a little warning—be careful not to toss back too many of these sweet treats, or you might end up wearing nothing more than a party hat.

1   ounce vanilla vodka
1   ounce Frangelica
1   ounce pineapple juice
1   ounce cranberry juice
    Ice cubes
    Sugar, to coat rim of glass
    Shaved coconut, for garnish

Combine all the ingredients in a drink shaker, and shake gently twice. Rim a glass with the sugar and add ice cubes. Pour over ice and garnish with the shaved coconut.

CARAMEL COWBOY

⟶ SERVES 1 ⟵

My sister Amanda lives in California. I don't always take her advice, but she's never shy about giving it. Truth is, she's often right, especially when it comes to what's hot and what's not. Amanda and her gal pals are getting tired of frou-frou martinis, so they've begun sipping the bubbly. The Caramel Cowboy they've come up with is an elegant cocktail that's flavorful and refreshing, without the heaviness that comes from a liquor-based drink. On this I certainly agree: From Cowtown to California, every lady looks a little more Hollywood glam with a champagne flute in her hand.

½   ounce Amaretto
½   ounce butterscotch schnapps
    Champagne, to fill flute
    Fresh mint sprig, for garnish

Pour the Amaretto and butterscotch schnapps into a champagne flute, and top with champagne. Garnish with the mint sprig.

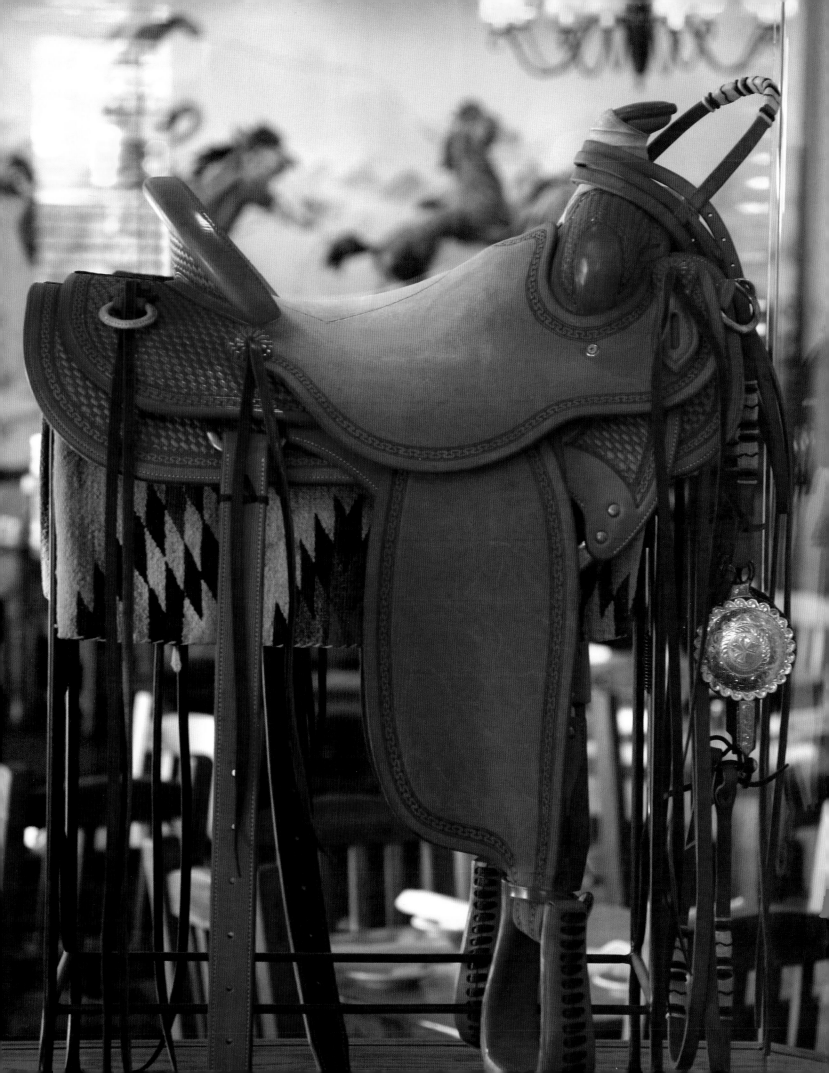

CF CHERRY LIMEADE

Living with a Sonic Drive-In within spitting distance makes our string of 100-degree summer days a little more bearable. There really is nothing quite like an ice-cold Route 44 cherry limeade to wipe the sweat off your brow and quench your thirst. As our most popular signature drink, the CF Cherry Limeade is always garnished with a maraschino cherry.

2 ounces cherry vodka
1/4 ounce Grenadine
1/4 ounce Rose's lime juice
2 ounces Sweet and Sour Mix (page 156)
2 ounces Sprite
Ice cubes
Lime wedge, for garnish
Maraschino cherry, for garnish

Add all the ingredients to a glass filled with ice, and stir gently. Garnish with the lime wedge and maraschino cherry.

COWGIRL COSMOPOLITAN

→→ SERVES 1 →→

We know that real cowgirls out on the ranch may not drink sissy cocktails. But in the big cities of Texas, there's a special type of gal who wears business suits by day and dresses like a rodeo queen on the weekends. When all gussied up for a night out in Cowtown, these ladies could stomp their boots all over those four from *Sex in the City*.

2 ounces orange vodka
1/4 ounce orange liqueur
3 ounces cranberry juice
Squeeze of lime
Twist of lemon, for garnish

Combine all the ingredients in a drink shaker, and shake vigorously. Strain into a martini glass, and garnish with the lemon twist.

KOSHER PICKLE MARTINI

Dirty isn't just for dancing, or for rolling up your sleeves and working in the barn. At Reata, we've tipped our hat to the dirty martini with a zesty drink that gives a powerful punch through the perfect use of pickles. We personally prefer using Claussen pickles, as we think they've got just the right combination of garlic and spices for the perkiest pucker.

1½ ounces vodka
1½ ounces pickle juice
    Pickle spear, for garnish

Combine all the ingredients over ice in a drink shaker, and shake vigorously. Strain into a martini glass, and garnish with the pickle spear.

MICALLEF MELONRITA

One of Reata's newest drinks, the Micallef Melonrita was developed as a refreshing complement to our summertime rooftop crawfish boil. The secret of getting the most flavor from your fruit is in the muddling, which means you firmly crush the watermelon with a long spoon.

2 (2-inch) cubes watermelon
1½ ounces tequila
½ ounce Tuaca
2 ounces Sweet and Sour Mix (page 156)
    Sugar, to coat rim of glass
    Ice cubes
    Watermelon wedge, for garnish

Combine all the ingredients in a drink shaker. Muddle the watermelon in the bottom of the shaker, and shake gently twice. Rim a glass with the sugar, and add ice cubes, Pour over ice and garnish with the watermelon wedge.

REATA BLOODY MARY

After a big night on the town, you better hail a few of these Marys in the hopes that this hair of the dog might bring some relief. For the maximum Mary, try using a pepper-infused vodka alongside the jalapeño garnish.

Salt, to coat rim of glass
Ice cubes
5 ounces Bloody Mary Mix
2 ounces vodka
Jalapeño pepper, for garnish

Salt the rim of a glass and add ice cubes. Add the Bloody Mary Mix, top with the vodka, and stir well. Garnish with the jalapeño.

Bloody Mary Mix

MAKES 5 CUPS

1 quart tomato juice
6 ounces Worcestershire sauce
1 ounce lemon juice
1 tablespoon Tabasco sauce
1 tablespoon red pepper flakes
1 tablespoon cracked black pepper
2 teaspoons chopped fresh dill, or 1 teaspoon dried dill
1/4 cup fresh horseradish, grated

Combine all the ingredients in a blender. Blend on high for 1 minute. Pour into airtight container and refrigerate. Mix will keep for two days in refrigerator.

SWEET AND SOUR MIX

Every bartender's staple, this mix is super easy to make and so much better than the store-bought brands. The secret to ours is using a cinnamon stick to layer flavors of sweet with depths of spice.

3 cups sugar
4 cups water
1 cinnamon stick
1 1/2 cups lime juice, preferably fresh squeezed

In a large saucepan, combine the sugar, water, and cinnamon, stirring until the sugar has dissolved. Bring to a boil over medium-high heat, then lower the heat, add the lime juice, and simmer for 5 minutes. Remove from the heat and let cool. When cool, remove the cinnamon stick. Store in an airtight container and refrigerate.

TEXAS TORNADO AZUL

We at Reata have learned a lot from the tornado that struck the original Fort Worth restaurant in the Bank One Tower. Now, we never forget to take a moment to sit back and enjoy the big wide-open Texas skies.

2   ounces tequila
1/2 ounce Blue Curacao
3   ounces Sweet and Sour Mix (page 156)
1/4 ounce orange juice, preferably fresh sqeeezed
     Squeeze of lime
     Salt, to coat rim of glass
     Ice cubes
     Lime wedge, for garnish

Combine all the ingredients in a drink shaker, and shake gently twice. Rim a glass with the salt, and add ice cubes. Pour over ice, and garnish with the lime wedge.

REATA GRAND

Life is good, but when fresh limes combine with aged tequila and citrus liqueur, life becomes downright grand. Whether you sip or slurp, gulp or guzzle, there's something about a grand margarita that makes what's big become little, what's hard become easy, and what's wrong become right.

2 ounces top shelf anejo tequila
1 ounce orange liqueur
3 ounces Sweet and Sour Mix (page 156)
½ ounce fresh orange juice
Squeeze of lime
Salt, to coat rim of glass
Ice cubes
Lime wedge, for garnish

Combine all the ingredients in a drink shaker, and shake gently twice. Rim a glass with the salt, and add ice cubes. Pour over ice and garnish with the lime wedge.

SPINDLETOP

To many Americans, Texas is all about oil, or "black gold." But here the black gold is the black coffee, and the drink is named for the huge oil strike that turned Beaumont into a boomtown back in 1900.

1 ounce amaretto
½ ounce Triple Sec
Splash of cinnamon schnapps
6 ounces coffee, freshly brewed and pipin' hot
Whipped cream, for garnish
Ground cinnamon, for garnish

Combine the amaretto, Triple Sec, and coffee in coffee mug. Add the schnapps and stir once. Top with the whipped cream, and sprinkle with the ground cinnamon.

ACKNOWLEDGMENTS

CONTRIBUTING AUTHORS

MIKE MICALLEF is the president of the Reata Restaurant locations in Fort Worth and Alpine, as well as the picturesque CF Ranch, a favorite subject for his camera. Mike tested, and in some cases retested, every recipe in this collection himself. This is his first cookbook. Mike readily acknowledges that he is only a small part of a big team at Reata. He would like to praise all the hard work that Tod Lewis, Russell Kirkpatrick, and Misti Callicott performed in producing the recipes for this cookbook. Mike would also like to recognize our group of fine chefs at Reata, including Juan Jaramillo, Fred Hamilton, Juan Rodriguez, and Travis Purdin.

JOHN DEMERS is the former food editor of the United Press International, the former editor of *Texas Foodlover*, and host of *Delicious Mischief* on Houston's CNN 650. He has authored or coauthored nearly forty books—most recently *Follow the Smoke: 14,783 Miles of Great Texas Barbecue.*

JULIE HATCH, a part of the Reata family since 2000, is a freelance writer and the owner of Creative Communications. With more than twenty years of professional communications experience to her credit, this is Julie's first cookbook.

CONTRIBUTING PHOTOGRAPHERS

LAURIE SMITH is a freelance photographer specializing in food and travel photography. Her assignments have taken her from Appalachia to India, and her  work on *Pastry Queen Christmas* by Rebecca Rather helped earn a 2007 James Beard Award. Laurie lives in Denver, Colorado.

GIL BARTEE is our Vice President of Development and an avid photographer. Gil has worked  as a photographic anthropologist in South America and Puerto Rico and has had his work published in a variety of publications. A large selection of Gil's photos can be found on www.sierralarena .com.

 KEN DAVIS is a former Reata employee and board member, a part-time photographer, and a full-time good friend. His current job title is "semi-retired." His most important role. . . Grand Dad.

RHONDA HOLE is a Fort Worth, Texas, based photographer specializing in commercial  photography, portraiture, and fine art. Her photographs routinely appear in national and regional magazines, books, websites, and brochures, and her original artwork resides in private collections worldwide.

LEO WESSON is a professional photographer and videographer based in Fort Worth with  special interests in cooking and traveling.

FOOD STYLING

ERICA McNEISH is a freelance photo stylist specializing in food. A former caterer and event 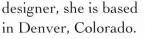 designer, she is based in Denver, Colorado.

INDEX